Sir Robert Peel
1788–1850
A Bibliography

Sir Robert Peel
1788–1850

A Bibliography

Leonard W. Cowie

BIBLIOGRAPHIES OF
BRITISH STATESMEN, NUMBER 13

GREGORY PALMER, SERIES EDITOR

Greenwood Press
Westport, Connecticut • London

Library of Congress Cataloging-in-Publication Data

Cowie, Leonard W.
    Sir Robert Peel, 1788–1850 : a bibliography / compiled by Leonard
W. Cowie.
        p.   cm.—(Bibliographies of British statesmen, ISSN
1056–5515 ; no. 13)
    Includes indexes.
    ISBN 0–313–29447–X (alk. paper)
    1. Peel, Robert, Sir, 1788–1850—Bibliography.   2. Great Britain—
Politics and government—19th century—Bibliography.   I. Title.
II. Series.
Z8667.8.C69   1996
[DA536.P3]
016.94107'3'092—dc20   95–41985

British Library Cataloguing in Publication Data is available.

Library of Congress Catalog Card Number: 95–41985
ISBN: 0–313–29447–X
ISSN: 1056–5515

First published in 1996

Greenwood Press, 88 Post Road West, Westport, CT 06881
An imprint of Greenwood Publishing Group, Inc.

Printed in the United States of America

∞™

The paper used in this book complies with the
Permanent Paper Standard issued by the National
Information Standards Organization (Z39.48–1984).

10 9 8 7 6 5 4 3 2 1

Contents

vi.   Contents

Introduction

Sir Robert Peel (1788-1855) was the son of a prosperous
Lancashire cotton-manufacturer and politician. Educated at
Harrow School and Oxford University, he entered Parliament as a
Tory in 1809. He held his first important post as Chief
Secretary for Ireland between 1812 and 1818, and between 1822
and 1830 he was, except for a brief period, Home Secretary, when
his most important achievement was the establishment of the
London police force in 1829. In 1830 the Whigs gained office,
pledged to accomplish parliamentary reform, and remained in
power nearly all the time until 1841. Peel strongly opposed the
Reform Bill of 1832, but when it was passed he acquiesced in it
and developed a Conservative party able to take advantage of the
changed circumstances. He became Prime Minister in 1841 and
showed himself unexpectedly able in dealing with imperial and
foreign issues. In India the threatening province of Sind was
occupied, and in North America the Oregon dispute was settled
with the United States. Although he had won the election as a
protectionist, the important feature of his administration was
a steady reduction of import duties, which he counterbalanced
by the introduction of a direct income tax in 1842. The
suffering caused by the famine in Ireland made him decide that
the Corn Laws must be repealed. He succeeded in doing this in
1846, but a resentful majority in his party secured his defeat
on another measure immediately afterwards . He resigned and
never held office again. In 1850 he died after being thrown from
his horse when out riding.

A brilliant parliamentarian and able administrator, he was
ready to change his mind when he considered this was required in
the interest of the nation, which produced divisions in his
party. Nevertheless, it may truly be said of him that he was the
creator of the modern Conservative party and (through his
followers - the Peelites) of the Liberal party as well.

This bibliography is concerned with these aspects of Peel's
life and work. The first two following sections provide a guide
to this. The Biographical Essay provides an outline of his life
and the policies which he adopted towards the problems facing
him. The Chronology sets out the important events of his life
together with the relevant national and international
occurrences of the time.

The section of Manuscript and Archival Resources gives the
location of the various collections of papers relating to Peel
and indicate which are the most important of them. It includes
also the relevant publications of the Historical Manuscripts

Commission. This is followed by a list of such catalogues and guides as have been chosen to indicate material about Peel. Finally, there is a descriptive list of Contemporary Newspapers and Journals.

The section on Published Resources provides a list of relevant bibliographies, biographies and studies of Peel and articles and essays upon him. These are arranged in chronological order of publication; but the concluding diaries, memoirs and letters are arranged alphabetically according to the names of their authors. Finally, there is a section on relevant Periodicals.

The section on Parliamentary Papers and Debates contains the most important papers concerning Peel together with sources for the debates in which he took part and his collected speeches.

The section on the Contemporaries of Peel is concerned with the leading people with whom he came into contact during his life and work. For each of them there is a brief biographical note and an indication of the most important material about them; and their connection with Peel and their relationship with him is explained.

The section on the Political Background explains, from the point of view of British politics, the nature of the seven important issues in which Peel was involved - the maintenance of law and order; the cause of reform; the position of the Church of England; the Bank of England; imperial and foreign policy in Europe, India and North America; the struggle over the Corn Laws; and the role of the Peelites before and after his death.

The section on Peel's Life and Career, which is arranged in chronological order, gives precise information with regard to leading events in both primary and secondary sources. This includes both material which has already been described and material mentioned in it for the first time.

The section on the Contemporary Portraits of Peel gives short accounts of these; and a Bibliography enables the descriptions of the many Caricatures of him to be found. The Places Associated with Peel are those in which he lived, studied, visited or worked. His connection with each of them is explained together with its location and present condition.

Abbreviations

AR   A.A.W. Ramsay, <u>Sir Robert Peel</u>
(no. 204)

BL   British Library

CCD   J.W. Croker, <u>Correspondence and Diaries</u>
(no. 285)

CSP   C.S. Parker, <u>Sir Robert Peel</u>
(no. 200)

CUP   Cambridge University Press

GM   <u>Greville Memoirs</u>
(no. 297)

HMSO   Her Majesty's Stationary Office

LP   Lawrence Peel, <u>Sketch of Sir Robert Peel</u>
(no. 193)

LV   <u>Letters of Queen Victoria</u>
(no. 312)

MC   Lord Mahon & E. Cardwell, <u>Peel's Memoirs</u>
(no. 194)

NG1   Norman Gash, <u>Mr. Secretary Peel</u>
(no. 215)

NG2   Norman Gash, <u>Sir Robert Peel</u>
(no. 216)

OUP   Oxford University Press

PD   <u>Parliamentary Debates</u>
(no. 323)

PH   <u>Parliamentary History</u>
(no. 322)

SPCK   Society for Promoting Christian Knowledge

SRP   <u>Speeches of Sir Robert Peel</u>
        (no. 325)

        Unless otherwise mentioned, books are published in
        London.

Biographical Essay

The long rule of 'King Cotton' began in British economic life during the eighteenth century. It pioneered the Industrial Revolution, which transformed Britain into the leading manufacturing country in the world. Cotton goods were the largest British exports, and the cotton mills were the first factories to come into existence.

The centre of the cotton industry was the county of Lancashire. Its humid atmosphere was highly suitable for both spinning and weaving. The ports were well-placed for the importation of raw cotton from America. It had a supply of free labour uninhibited by old guild regulations or traditions. And it had adventurous capitalists and inventors, who were ready and able to devise and adopt new means of production and organization which made manufacturing possible on an increasingly larger and more profitable scale. They produced men of wealth and ability who were able to take part in the life and government of the country.

One of these was Sir Robert Peel, the first Prime Minister to come from a commercial family. He was the grandson of the first Robert Peel (1723-1795), who moved into industry from the middle-class farming in which the family had hitherto been engaged. Inheriting the farmhouse of Peel Fold (see no. 631), he set up cotton looms in the 'housepart' of the building. Later he saw the value of the newly-invented method of printing on calico (plain white cotton cloth) and joined with partners to set up a calico-printing works at Brookside, near to Peel Fold, to which were added spinning and weaving mills that used all the new mechanical inventions. One of his patterns was a parsley-leaf design, which gained him the nickname of 'Parsley.' After some years his partners moved to Bury, and he remained on his own at Brookside until it was attacked by rioting 'Luddites' (machine-wreckers) in 1779. He removed to Burton-on-Trent in Staffordshire, where he built three mills and a canal. He became yet more prosperous, but did not seek any power or prestige beyond his commercial undertakings (see no. 668).

His third son, Robert (1750-1830), combined his father's energetic and capable commercial ability with an interest in public life and responsibility. In about 1773 he joined his father's former partners at their factory near Bury. In 1783 he married Ellen Yates, the daughter of one of his partners. They resided in Chamber Hall, near to the works (see no. 632) and had nine children. By the end of the century, he was one of the wealthiest cotton-manufacturers in the whole kingdom. His partners had died or retired. He was in sole control of the business, employing some 15,000 people in his mills and factories.

By then he had embarked upon his political career. He had bought land which gave him possession of the pocket-borough of Tamworth, and in 1790 he became one of its representatives in Parliament. He had become also a landed gentleman in 1796 when he bought and rebuilt the nearby manor house of Drayton (see no. 633). Two years after he became a Member of Parliament, Britain entered upon the long war against France. He formed volunteer forces in Lancashire and Staffordshire, and when the Prime Minister, the Younger Pitt, asked the country for contributions to help the war effort, he donated £10,000. These acts of patriotism led him to being made a baronet in 1800.

As a Member of Parliament he initiated legislation which affected the cotton industry. Children were extensively employed in the cotton mills. Their labour was cheap, and their small stature enabled them to move easily among the machines to perform various tasks. He had begun the plan of bringing pauper children from the London workhouses to labour in his undertakings. At one time he employed nearly a thousand of these children, and now other mill-owners engaged them. He became aware of the need to protect them against exploitation by their employers and in 1802 secured the passing of an Act which limited the working hours of these 'parish apprentices; and when changing circumstances replaced them by 'free' children hired out by their parents, he was instrumental in passing an Act in 1819 which limited the age of employment of such children to nine years and the working-day to twelve hours and made provision for their clothing, education and conditions of labour (see no. 757). These measures were not, in fact, very effective; the need for factory inspectors to enforce such regulations had not yet been realized; but it did accept the need for intervention by the government to improve industrial working conditions and was the first of a succession of subsequent increasingly effective and beneficial factory acts.

His first two children were daughters, and then in 1788 his first son was born at Chamber Hall (see no. 632) and was christened Robert. He was delighted to have a son and seems to have wanted him to have a political career. The boy was first taught at a small school kept by the Vicar of Tamworth. Where was he then to go? His grandfather and father had been educated at Blackburn Grammar School, but his father had other plans for him. Of schools with a national reputation by then, Harrow had achieved an eminent position under its headmaster, Dr. Joseph Drury (see no. 634). The boy was accordingly sent there in 1800 and soon became friendly with Byron, the future poet, who was a schoolfellow there. At first he was at a disadvantage; he had not learnt Latin versification at Tamworth and was kept back until he mastered this essential requirement; but thereafter he did so well that his tutor said, 'You boys will one day see Peel Prime Minister!'

The next stage in his education was to be one of the two universities then existing in England - Oxford or Cambridge. Oxford by this time had gained a progressive image through its reform of the degree system. The list of subjects taught had been divided into two faculties or 'schools' - Literae Humaniores' (which included both Classical literature and

Philosophy) and Mathematics (which included Physics). These were examined - though still mainly orally - at the end of the course, and the successful candidates obtained a first or second class degree. Undergraduates might submit themselves for examination in either <u>Literae Humaniores</u> or both.

Prominent in securing these reforms was Cyril Jackson, Dean of Christ Church, who had also given it an unrivalled intellectual reputation among the colleges. The young Robert Peel was accordingly sent there in 1805. Jackson was a strict disciplinarian and especially devoted his energies to the advancement of the most promising students of the college. Among these was Peel, who was told by Jackson to 'work like a tiger or like a dragon, if dragons work more and harder than tigers.' This he did and devoted, it was said, eighteen hours a day to his studies in his final year; and he owed much to the direction of his tutor, Charles Lloyd, who later became Bishop of Oxford (see no. 784). He decided to take both schools and in 1808 was placed in the first class in both. He was not merely the only candidate to be awarded this distinction that year but also the first since the schools had been divided and classes had been granted.

After taking his degree, Peel studied law at Lincoln's Inn in London, but he was not to follow a legal career. In 1809 his father bought for him an Irish pocket borough, the city of Cashel, in the county of Tipperary, and he was returned to the House of Commons as its M.P. He entered Parliament, like his father, as a Tory, and then a Tory government under Spencer Perceval was in power. Parliamentary custom decrees that the reply to the King's speech at the opening of each session should be made by a backbencher; and at the opening of the session in January 1810 Peel was invited to do this, and his speech brought him universal praise (see no. 706). Among those whom he impressed was Lord Liverpool the Secretary for War and Colonies, and that summer he made him one of his Under Secretaries. It was customary at this time for the Colonial Secretary also to be Secretary <u>for</u> War, whose duty was to prepare the general policy of the department and to direct the military operations of war. There was also a Secretary <u>at</u> War, who exercised most of the military functions of the present-day Ministry of Defence.

After holding this post for two years, Peel's political position suddenly changed. In May 1812 a madman shot the Prime Minister dead in the lobby of the House of Commons. He was succeeded by Lord Liverpool, who, though not entirely willingly (see no. 710), appointed Peel to be Chief Secretary for Ireland. The nominal head of the government of Ireland, as had been established by the Act of Union of 1801, was the Lord-Lieutenant, but he had largely a dignified ceremonial function the representative of the Crown and resided permanently in Dublin. The actual head of the administration was the Chief Secretary, and he was responsible to Parliament for his actions. Peel was only partly resident in Dublin; when Parliament was sitting he had to be in London, and crossing St. George's Channel in the sailing packet-boats of those days was not always pleasant (see no. 740).

Ireland, then as now, was an island whose people were divided in religion and politics, a situation which the Act of Union had exacerbated rather then relieved. The tie with Britain was liked by the Protestants, who were mainly in the north and formed about a quarter of the population, but they were opposed by the rest of the population, who were Roman Catholics. Union had not, as the Younger Pitt intended it should, been accompanied by Roman Catholic Emancipation. This meant that Roman Catholics in Ireland, though allowed to vote, could not sit in the Parliament of the United Kingdom. The Act of Union had been passed mainly in the interest of British safety in wartime, and Peel belived, as did most British politicians, it was still necessary for the protection of Britain. He opposed the extension of political rights to Roman Catholics because he thought it would threaten British rule over the island. This brought him into conflict with the leader of the movement for Roman Catholic Emancipation, Daniel O'Connell, who called him 'Orange Peel' in relation to the Orange Lodges (called after the Dutch William of Organge, who became King William III and defeated the Roman Catholic King James II in Ireland), which supported the Protestant cause, and a bitter quarrel ensued between the two men (see nos. 731-738).

O'Connell's campaign added to the violence and lawlessness which was already endemic in Ireland, and Peel's policy had to be dominated by the need to restore law and order. His main effort in this direction was embodied in the Peace Preservation Act and the Insurrection Act both passed in 1814, which for the first time in Ireland established professional, salaried magistrates and full-time local police forces (see nos. 722-724). The Police Preservation Force, as it came to be called, was the forerunner of both the Royal Irish Constabulary and the Metropolitan Police Force, which he established in London fifteen years later.

On becoming Chief Secretary, Peel had thought it advisable not to continue in his Irish seat, and his father this time bought him an English borough - Chippenham in Wiltshire. His parliamentary reputation was advanced in May 1817 when, during a debate on the laws affecting Roman Catholics, he made an outstanding speech opposing emancipation. This gained him recognition as a strong supporter of the Protestant cause, which brought its reward the next month. In 1604 King James I had granted the universities of Oxford and Cambridge the privilege of each sending two members (known as burgesses) to Parliament. In June 1817 one of these places became vacant at Oxford. It had been supposed that Canning would secure it, but but the Masters of Arts of the University, who were the electors, preferred Peel, and he achieved this exalted position (see nos. 743-749).

A little over a year later, Peel resigned his Irish Secretaryship. He was tired of Ireland and its problems; he wanted to break from it all (see nos. 758-763). And his Irish post was isolated from the mainstream of British politics. His continuance in it made further promotion unlikely. When the time came, he wanted to have an active political career. Meanwhile, he gave his attention to the financial problems of the post-war years by accepting the Chairmanship of the Currency Commission and secured the resumption of cash payments by the Bank of England in 1819.

The next year he married Julia, the daughter of General Sir John Floyd, who was second-in-command of the army of Ireland during the greater part of his time there. The General had served in India, where Julia was born in 1785. As an acknowledged beauty, she had possessed many admirers, but after her marriage she devoted herself entirely to her husband and gave him the understanding and sympathy he needed in his exacting political life.

When George IV ascended the throne in the spring of 1820, he immediately required the ministry to set about dissolving

his unhappy marriage with Caroline of Brunswick. It began
proceedings against her reluctantly until popular support for her
compelled these to be withdrawn, but not before Canning had
resigned in 1821 from his post as President of the Board of Control
(of India) in protest against the treatment of the Queen.
Liverpool wished Peel to be his successor, but he refused (see
nos. 767-768). Early the next year, however, he was offered the
post of Home Secretary, which he accepted.

The Home Secretaryship has been described as 'one of the most
historic, interesting and demanding posts in the British
government.' Its functions have never been exactly defined. In
fact, its holder is responsible for those domestic matters which
have not been assigned specifically to other government
departments, and these include the upholding of public order and
the enforcement of the law. During the first period in which he
held this office, Peel successfully began a thorough reform of the
criminal law and the prison system as well as the repeal of the
Combination Laws, which had outlawed trade unions, in 1824.

In February 1827 Liverpool was incapacitated by a paralytic
stroke and had to resign. His successor was Canning, who came into
office the next April. Peel refused to serve under him because he
could not agree with the new Prime Minister's support for Roman
Catholic Emancipation (see nos. 787-793). Canning's health,
however, was not good. His ministry was destined to last for less
than six months. He died in the August of the same year.

George IV appointed to succeedd him Frederick John Robinson
(now Viscount Goderich), a weak man whom he hoped to be able to
dominate . Peel was not included in the ministry because the King
resented his unwillingness to serve in the previous government.
Goderich soon showed himself unfitted for the post. He was unable
to preserve unity among his colleagues, and in January 1828 he
resigned without ever facing Parliament.

The King now sent for the Duke of Wellington, who formed an
administration in which Peel came back to the Home Office. His
short period there was not an easy one for him. He had to accept
the repeal of the Test and Corporation Acts and Roman Catholic
Emancipation, which he had hitherto strongly opposed. This change
of attitude gained him the nickname of 'Spinning Jenny,' the
eighteenth-century machine for spinning a number of cotton
threads simultaneously. It resulted also in him being rejected by
the University of Oxford, and the party managers had to secure for
him the pocket borough of Westbury in Wiltshire. He was able,
however, to continue reforming the criminal law and to establish
the Metropolitan Police Force in which his name is still recalled
through the nickname of 'Bobbies' for policemen.

Henceforward Peel followed a policy of combining support for
the Church of England with religious toleration. Thus, when the
Nonconformists,who were excluded from Oxford and Cambridge,
formed University College in London, which was without religious
tests, he assisted the establishment of King's College as an
Anglican institution in the capital; but in 1835 he supported the
foundation of a federal University of London including these two
colleges and approved of its religious comprehension (see nos.
797-799, 895).

In May 1830 Peel's father died, and he inherited both the
baronetcy and Drayton Hall. The next month George IV died, and in
those day a monarch's death brought about the dissolution

of Parliament. In the ensuing general election Peel decided to
stand for Tamworth for which he was duly returned. The government
survived the election, but its religious legislation had left it
hopelessly divided. Moreover, it was now clear that there was a
growing desire for parliamentary reform in the country.
Wellington misread the situation. At the opening of Parliament in
1830 he made a defiant speech in defence of the established
constitution which aroused such opposition that it immediately
brought about the defeat and resignation of his
administration.

He was succeeded by Lord Grey at the head of a Whig government
which was united in intending to bring about parliamentary
reform. As a result of the carefully cautious attitude Peel
adopted towards the Reform Bill of 1832 (see nos. 847-851), the
Tories - now becoming known as Conservatives - were able to make an
unexpectedly early return to power. Grey retired in the summer of
1834 and was succeeded by Melbourne, but in the November of that
year disunity in his ministry led him to resign. Upon Wellington's
insistence, Peel, who was in Rome at the time, was immediately
summoned and on his return formed a ministry. He was able to begin
the reform of the Church of England with the establishment of the
Ecclesiastical Commission; but when there was a general election
in the spring of 1835, the Conservatives were unable to secure a
majority despite Peel's Tamworth Manifesto, and Peel once more
led the opposition (see nos. 877-885).

Melbourne became Prime Minister, but his ministry was weak,
and he needed Peel's help to secure the passing of the Municipal
Corporations Act of 1835, which reformed city and town
government. He survived, however, the general election brought
about by William IV's death, but continuing ministerial disunity
again brought about his resignation in May 1839. Peel proceeded to
form an administration and asked the young Queen Victoria to
dismiss those of her ladies of the bedchamber who were related to
the former Whig ministers. Victoria's unwillingness to part with
Melbourne and dislike of Peel made her persistently refuse to do
this.

The Queen persuaded Melbourne to remain in office, but his
government was increasingly unsuccessful. It was embarrassed by
the Chartist Manifesto of 1838, which demanded annual
parliaments, equal electoral districts, no property
qualification for Members of Parliament, voting by ballot and the
payment of Members of Parliament. The movement represented the
desire among the working class for political power in the face of
the prevailing economic distress and unemployment. Rejection by
Parliament of a Chartist petition in July 1839 resulted in
violence and disorder in several parts of the country. Melbourne
had finally to resign in June 1841. The Conservatives gained the
large majority of nearly a hundred at the resulting general
election, and the government resigned. This time, under the
moderating influence of Prince Albert, the Queen agreed to
dismiss three of her ladies when Peel took power.

The new administration immediately and inevitably inherited
many of the difficulties of its predecessor. The strength of the
Chartists in the country, however, began to decline notably after
Parliament rejected a second petition in May 1842; and Peel set
out at once on a varied programme of reform which met with
considerable success in assisting the revival of national
prosperity. The measures he was able to put into effect during

these years included the Budget of 1842, which was one of the most important of the nineteenth century with its reduction of duties on a large number of articles in general consumption that were imported from abroad and its introduction of an income tax, together with the control of paper money by the Bank Charter Act of 1844. In 1844 also a Factory Act limited the working day of women to 12 hours and of children aged 8 to 13 to 6½ hours. By then, however, Peel was facing difficulties caused by party dissensions over the Ten Hours clause and the Sugar Duties (see nos. 980 - 985, 1014 - 1016).

More serious and destined to be fatal to the ministry was the repeal of the Corn Laws, which was passed in 1846. This split the Conservatives and forced his immediate resignation. His supporters, the Peelites, became a separate parliamentary group, but he remained aloof from active participation in politics. He last attended the House of Commons on 28th. June 1850 when he spoke against Lord Palmerston's handling of the Don Pacifico affair. The next morning he went to a meeting of the commissioners for the proposed Great Exhibition in Hyde Park in 1851 and in the afternoon set out on his customary daily ride. At the top of Constitution Hill, his horse became restive and threw him to the ground. He was taken grievously injured home to Whitehall Gardens, where he died on 2nd. July. The government proposed he should have a tomb in Westminster Abbey, but in accordance with his wishes, as expressed in his will, he was interred in the family vault at Drayton Bassett Parish Church.

Chronology

5th. February 1788	birth of Robert Peel
1801-1804	at Harrow School
1804-1809	at Christ Church, Oxford
14th. April 1809	M.P. for Cashel
6th. September 1809	DUKE OF PORTLAND RESIGNED
4th. October 1809	SPENCER PERCEVAL PRIME MINISTER
31st. May 1810	Under-Secretary for War and Colonies
11th. May 1812	SPENCER PERCEVAL MURDERED
8th. June 1812	LORD LIVERPOOL PRIME MINISTER
30th. July 1812	Chief Secretary for Ireland
7th. October 1812	M.P. for Chippenham
18th. June 1815	BATTLE OF WATERLOO
9th. May 1817	R.C. Emancipation speech
3rd. June 1817	M.P. for Oxford University
18th. August 1817	resigned Irish Secretaryship
1st. - 25th. July 1818	GENERAL ELECTION
29th. January 1820	DEATH OF GEORGE III; ACCESSION OF GEORGE IV
6th. March - 14th.April 1820	GENERAL ELECTION
8th. June 1820	married Julia Floyd
17th. January 1822	Home Secretary

12th. May 1823	O'CONNELL FOUNDED CATHOLIC ASSOCIATION
12th April 1827	Refused to serve under Canning
9th. May 1828	TEST AND CORPORATION ACTS REPEALED
4th. July 1828	O'CONNELL M.P.FOR COUNTY CLARE
9th. February 1829	resigned seat for Oxford
27th. February & 1st. March 1829	ELECTION AT OXFORD
2nd. March 1829	M.P. for Westbury
13th. March 1829	R.C. RELIEF BILL PASSED
19th. June 1829	METROPOLITAN POLICE ESTABLISHED
17th. April 1830	his meeting with George IV
3rd. May 1830	death of his father
26th. June 1830	DEATH OF GEORGE IV; ACCESSION OF WILLIAM IV
1st. March 1831	FIRST REFORM BILL INTRODUCED INTO COMMONS
3rd. March 1831	his first speech on Reform Bill
21st. March 1831	COMMONS DEFEATED FIRST REFORM BILL
21st. September 1831	COMMONS PASSED SECOND REFORM BILL
7th. October 1831	LORDS DEFEATED SECOND REFORM BILL
12th. December 1831	THIRD REFORM BILL INTRODUCED INTO COMMONS
23rd. March 1832	COMMONS PASSED THIRD REFORM BILL
7th.- 14th. May 1832	THE DAYS OF MAY
7th. June 1832	LORDS PASSED THIRD REFORM BILL
9th. July 1834	GREY RESIGNED
16th. July 1834	MELBOURNE PRIME MINISTER
16th. October 1834	FIRE DAMAGED PARLIAMENT
14th. November 1834	MELBOURNE RESIGNED
15th.- 25th. November 1834	Hudson's journey to Rome

14   Sir Robert Peel

26th. November - 8th. December 1834	Peel's return to London
9th. December 1834	Prime Minister
18th. December 1834	Tamworth Manifesto
23rd. December 1834	Mansion House speech
4th. February 1835	ECCLESIASTICAL COMMISSION ISSUED
8th. April 1835	resigned Premiership
18th. April 1835	MELBOURNE PRIME MINISTER
9th. September 1835	MUNICIPAL CORPORATIONS ACT PASSED
20th. June 1837	DEATH OF WILLIAM IV; ACCESSION OF VICTORIA
29th. December 1837	U.S. STEAMER CAROLINE BURNT
18th. September 1838	ANTI-CORN LAW LEAGUE FORMED
7th. May 1839	MELBOURNE RESIGNED
13th. May 1839	MELBOURNE RETURNED AFTER BEDCHAMBER CRISIS
4th. September 1839	CHARTIST RISING IN NEWPORT
10th. February 1840	VICTORIA MARRIED ALBERT
28th. June 1841	election speech at Tamworth
30th. August 1841	Prime Minister
11th. March 1842	first free trade budget
3rd. May 1842	CHARTIST NATIONAL PETITION
20th. January 1843	EDWARD DRUMMOND MURDERED
19th. July 1844	BANK CHARTER ACT PASSED
13th. March 1845	converted to free trade by Cobden's speech
22nd. November 1845	Edinburgh Letter published
2nd. December 1845	announced his willingness to repeal Corn Laws
2nd. December 1845	resignation from Premiership
13th. December 1845	recalled on Russell's failure to form government

25th. June 1846	CORN BILL PASSED; IRISH COERCION BILL DEFEATED
29th. June 1846	resigned from Premiership
28th. June 1850	DON PACIFICO DEBATE
29TH. June 1850	thrown from his horse
2nd. July 1850	died
10th. July 1850	funeral
23rd. February 1852	RUSSELL RESIGNED; DERBY PRIME MINISTER
16th. December 1852	DISRAELI'S FIRST BUDGET DEFEATED
20th. December 1852	DERBY RESIGNED; ABERDEEN PRIME MINISTER
18th. April 1853	GLADSTONE'S FIRST BUDGET
28th. March 1854	BRITAIN DECLARED WAR ON RUSSIA
1st. February 1855	ABERDEEN RESIGNED
6th. February 1855	PALMERSTON PRIME MINISTER
30th. March 1856	TREATY OF PARIS (END OF CRIMEAN WAR
13th. April 1857	PALMERSTON WON GENERAL ELECTION
19th. February 1858	PALMERSTON RESIGNED
26th. February 1858	DERBY PRIME MINISTER
8th. June 1859	OPPOSITION MEETING IN WILLIS'S ROOMS
10th. June 1859	DERBY RESIGNED; PALMERSTON PRIME MINISTER

1

Manuscript and Archival Resources

LIBRARIES AND COLLECTIONS

1. National Register of Archives.

   The National Register of Archives, Quality House, Quality
Court, Chancery Lane, London WC2A 1HP has comprehensive
catalogues of many of the collections of non-governmental
records possessed by British archives and libraries, as well
as some American ones, and also information about conditions
of access to collections in private ownership. Where it has
catalogued a collection, the reference is given below in
brackets after the letters NRA.

2. National Inventory of Documentary Sources.

   A microfiche index, providing in some instances more information than in the National Register of Archives, has
been produced by Chadwyck-Healey Ltd. of Cambridge entitled
A National Inventory of Documentary Sources in the United
Kingdom. Some American research libraries have it.

3. Harvest Microform.

   A microfilm edition of Peel's working papers and letters,
as contained in the Additional Manuscripts of the British
Library, has been published by Harvester Press Microform
Publications Ltd. of Brighton, East Sussex.

BRITISH ISLES

British Library, London WC1B 2DG2

4. Peel Papers, Add. MSS. 40181-40617
5. Liverpool Papers, Add. MSS. 38109-38489
6. Bentham Papers, Add. MSS. 33537-33564
7. Huakisson Papers, Add. MSS. 38734-38770
8. Aberdeen Papers, Add. MSS. 453061-43065
   (correspondence with Peel 1828-1850)
9. Correspondence with W.E. Gladstone , Add. MSS. 44275-
   44650, Memoranda 44777
10. Correspondence with John Charles Herries 1824-1842,
    Add. MSS. 57402 (NRA 4798 Herries)
11. Correspondencve with Prince Lieven 1822-1834
    Add. MSS. 47291-47296

12. Letters to Sidney Smirke on buildings at Drayton,
    Add. MSS.59847
13. Correspondence with Lord Wellesley 1822-1842,
    Add. MSS. 37298-37313 passim

Public Record Office, Kew, Richmond
14. Colonial Office:
    C.O. 324/132 Correspondence 1810-1811
    C.O. 324/134 Correspondence 1811-1812
15. War Office:
    W.O. 6/29-30 Correspondence with Wellington 1810-1812
        6/50 Peninsular War
        6/122-123 General Correspondence 1810-1813
16. Home Office:
    H.O. 41/7-8 Disturbances 1821-1830
        43/31-39 Domestic Correspondence 1821-1830
        44/14-16 Miscellaneous Correspondence
        60/1 Police Entry Books 1821-1830
        61/1-2 Metropolitan Police 1820-1830
        63/11 Police and Secret Service 1827-1831
        100/211 Ireland, Miscellaneous Letters
17. Close Rolls:
    C 54/7308
18. Cardwell Papers:
    Correspondence with Goulburn GD, 48-50
    Notes on Peel Papers and material for a life of Peel
    1834-1835, GD48/53
19. Ellenborough Papers:
    Journal 1834-1835, 1837-1838, 1841, 30/12/28/5-7
    Correspondence with Peel 1829-1847, 30/12/21/1;
    30/12/29 pt. 1/18; 30/12/29 pt. 2/9; 30/12/4/29
    (NRA 21870 Law - PRO 30/12)
    Political Correspondence 1835-1861, 30/12/6/6
    Letters to Ellenborough 1841-1844,30/12/37
20. Correspondence with Sir George Murray 1828-1846
    (NRA 28811 Murray - WO80)
21. Correspondence with Lord John Russell 1836-1850,
    30/22/7; 30/228 pt. 1 (NRA 8659 Russell - PRO 30/22)

Royal Archives, Windsor
22. Queen Victoria's Journal
23. Correspondence of Peel with Queen Victoria, Prince Albert
    and George Anson 1841-1850
24. Memoranda by Prince Albert and George Anson
25. Correspondence and Papers on:
    Change of Government 1841
    Irish Policy 1844-1846
    Ministerial Crisis December 1845
    Peel's policy and change of government 1846
    Formation of Russell's administration
26. Baron Stockmar's Papers

Scottish Record Office, Edinburgh
27. Correspondence with Sir George Clerk 1830-1847
    (NRA 21982 Clerk - GD18)
28. Correspondence with the First Marquess of Dalhousie 1843-
    1846 (NRA 17164 Ramsay - GD45. See also NRA (S) 0805)
29. Correspondence with the Earl of Haddington c1830-1850
    (NRA 10114 Hamilton - GD249. See also NRA S 010)

30. Letters to G.W. Hope 1842-1848   (NRA 10172 Hope GD364.
    See also NRA S 0485)
31. Letters to Sir Charles Augustus Murray 1841-1844 (NRA
    14153 Murray - GD261. See also NRA S 0485)
32. Letters to R.A. Nisbet-Hamilton 1830-1841 (NRA 34282
    Ogilvy - GD205/box 46)
33. Letters among the Winton House Papers 1830-1841.
    Annual Report, 1963, App. 6

National Library of Scotland,Edinburgh
34. Correspondence with Sir Thomas Cochrane 1835-1842
35. Correspondence with Sir Edward Ellice (NRA 883 Ellice,
    MS15047. See also NRA S 1968)
36. Correspondence with Sir Walter Scott 182-1830,
    MSS 3895-3913 passim

National Register of Archives (Scotland), Edinburgh
37. Letters to Sir John and Sir George Sinclair 1820-1840
    (NRA 10552 Sinclair, vols. 5, 17. See also NRA S 0189)
38. Letters to John Swinton (NRA 10561 Swinton. See also NRA
    S 0200)

State Paper Office, Dublin
39. Private Official Letters 1811-1823
40. General Private Correspondence 1804-1814 & 1814-1821
41. Official Papers, Second Series: Military; Privy Council;
    Finance; Trade and Industries
42. State of Country Series I, 1796-1831: MS Calendar;
    Correspondence
43. Irish Privy Council Minute Books 1812-1818

National Library, Dublin
44. Richmond Papers: Letters and Papers of the Fourth
    Duke of Richmond

Royal Irish Academy, Dublin
45. MS Diary of Mr. Justice Day

Public Record Office of Northern Ireland, Belfast
46. Correspondence with First Marquis of Anglesey
    (NRA 10 - D619/26B)
47. Letters to J.L. Foster 1813-1840 (NRA 6701 Skeffington
    - T2519/7)
48. Correspondence with John Foster 1813-1823
    (NRA Skeffington D207/39)
49. Correspondence with Sir G.F. Hill and G.R. Dawson 1812-
    1829 (NRA 19000 Hill - D426)

County Museum,Armagh
50. Blacker Autobiography:
    Written by c1840 by Lt. Col. William Blacker (1777-1855),
    High Sheriff for County Armagh and Vice-Treasurer of
    Ireland 1817-1829.

Buckinghamshire Record Office, Aylesbury
51. Letters to First Baron Cottesloe 1840-1846
    (NRA 15283 Fremantle - D/FR)

Cambridge University Library, Department of Manuscripts and
University Archives
52. Cambridge University Reporter, 12/5/1965, pl. 80

Fitzwilliam Museum, Cambridge
53. Correspondence mainly with Artists 1823-1850
    (NRA 22840 Peel)

Trinity College, Cambridge
54. Letters to Lord Houghton HM Corresp. file 19/2/1987

Cumbria Record Office, Carlisle
55. Correspondence with Sir James Graham (NRA 2634 Graham)

Durham County Record Office
56. Letters to Third Marquess of Londonderry 1826-1849
    (NRA 11528 Vane-Tempest-Stewart, pp. 170, 177)

Exeter Cathedral Library
57. Letters to Henry Phillpotts (NRA 25909 Phillpotts)

Rt. Hon.the Earl of Harrowby, Sandon Hall, Staffordshire
58. Correspondence with First and Second Earls of Harrowby,
    Lord Dudley Coutts Stuart and William Collins 1832-1850
    (NRA 1561 Ryder)

St. Deiniol's Library, Hawarden
59. Correspondence with Sir John Gladstone (NRA 14174
    Gladstone - 303, 361-362)
60. Corresponcence with Fifth Duke of Newcastle 1842-1843
    (NRA 14174 Gladstone, p. 18)

Port Eliot, St. Germans, Cornwall
61. Letters to Third Earl of St. Germans 1841-1847
    (NRA 28659 Eliot - HMC)

Glamorgan Record Office, Cardiff
62. Correspondence mainly with Lord Lyndhurst 1830-1848
    (NRA 11640 Copley, pp. 33-35, 45, 62)

Hughenden Manor, High Wycombe, Buckinghamshire
63. Disraeli Papers (commonly called the Hughenden Papers)

India Office Library and Records, London SE1 8NG
64. Letters to LOrd Tweeddale (NRA 17520 Hay - MSS. Eur. F96)

Keele University Library
65. Correspondence with Second Earl of Kildare
    (NRA 1248 Sneyd - Additional)

Kent Archives Office, Maidstone
66. Correspondence and Papers 1843-1848 (NRA Stanhope
    - U1590/S4)
67. Correspondence with First and Second Marquesses Camden
    (NRA 8410 Pratt - U840/C208, 250, 411)
68. Correspondence with First Viscount Hardinge 1844-1847
    (NRA 5379 Hardinge - MSS. Eur. E389)
69. Letters to Sir Edward and Wyndham Knatchbull 1828-1845
    (NRA Knatchbull - U951 C14)

70. Letters to Lord Mahon (1821-1850) (NRA 25095 Stanhope - U1590/S4)

71. Letters to Lord Whitworth 1813-1818 (NRA Sackville - U269/0225)

Lambeth Palace Library
72. Correspondence with Christopher Wordsworth 1834-1844, MSS. 1822, 2148

Imperial College, London University
73. Letters to William Buckland 1842-1852
    (NRA 11556 Playfair)
74. Letters to First Baron Playfair 1842-1850
    (NRA 11556 Playfair)

University College Manuscripts Room, London University,
75. Correspondence with Sir Edwin Chadwick 1841-1846
    (NRA 21653 Chadwick)
76. Letters to Sir Joseph Parkes on drainage matters
    1844-1848 (NRA 6318 Parkes, p. 3)

Royal Academy of Arts, London
77. Letters to Sir Thomas Lawrence 1824-1829
    (NRA 14837 Royal Academy)

Manchester Central Library
78. Letters to J.F. Foster 1829-1830, Stipendiary
    Magistrate, Manchester

Multiple Locations
79. Correspondence with Maurice Fitzgerald 1813-1846
    (NRA 29433 Fitzgerald)
80. Correspondence with Lord Lyttleton (NRA 14545
    Lyttleton, no. 9)
81. Letters to Baron Neumann c1833-1849 (NRA 6823
    Codrington, vol. 2, p. 68)

Norfolk Record Office, Norwich
82. Letters to Sir Henry Bulwer 1842-1849 (NRA 6790
    Bulwer, p. 5)

His Grace the Duke of Northumberland, Alnwick Castle
83. Letters to Henry Drummond 1836-1850 (NRA 836 Percy)

Nottingham University Library
84. Correspondence with the Fourth and Fifth Dukes of
    Newcastle 1810-1848
    (NRA 7411 Pelham, pp. 36, 40, 45-7, 62, 76)

Bodleian Library, Oxford, Department of Western Manuscripts
85. Correspondence with Benjamin Disraeli 1841-1846
    (NRA 842 Disraeli - MSS Disraeli)
86. Correspondence with Sir Thomas Phillips 1825-1842
    (NRA 26260 Phillips - MSS Phillips-Robinson)
87. Correspondence with Samual Wilberforce 1836-1848
    (NRA 7132 Wilberforce - MSS Wilberforce; Don E 164-165)
88. Miscellaneous Letters, Accessions to Repositories, 1967

Taylor Institution Library,Oxford
89. Letters from members of Peel's family
    (NRA 11664 Taylor Institution)

Christ Church, Oxford
90. Siga. 1806-1823
91. Collections Book 1789-1814
92. Battels 1805-1809
93. Various pamphlets and other items

Mr. G.F. Peel
94. Peel MSS
    Personal letters and other items relating to Sir Robert and
Lady Peel not among the political papers in the British
Library. After the original collection was fully used by
George Peel in The Private Letters of Sir Robert Peel
(no. 202), most of it was destroyed by enemy bombing in London
in 1940.

Sheffield City Libraries, Archive Division
95. Letters to First and Second Barons Wharncliffe
    1831-1844 (NRA 1077 Montagu-Stuart)

Southampton University Library
96. Letters to Lord Palmerston 1823-1841 (NRA 12889 Temple)
97. Letters to Duke of Wellington 1827-1846
    (NRA 20085 Wellesley)

Staffordshire Record Office, Stafford
98. Letters to William and Richard Dyott 1826-1833
    (NRA 9000 Dyott - 10/1/10)

Surrey Record Office, Kingston upon Thames
99. Goulburn Papers:
    Correspondence with Peel 13/2
    Account, cheque, commonplace and note books relating to
    Sir Robert and Lady Peel and the Peel estate
    (NRA 777 Goulburn)

Tamworth Public Library
100. Mitchell Collection:
    Volumes of news-cuttings and miscellaneous items about
    the history of Tamworth and district.

Wiltshire Record Office, Trowbridge
101. Correspondence with Sidney Herbert
    (NRA 22080 Herbert - 1422, 2057)

Borthwick Institute of Historical Research, York University
102. Letters to First Viscount Halifax 1846-1850
    (NRA 8128 Wood A4/122)

West Sussex Record Office, Chichester
103. Letters to Fourth and Fifth Dukes of Richmond 1825-1847
    (NRA 850 Gordon Lennox - Add. MSS. 5424-5426)

West Yorkshire Record Office, Doncaster
104. Correspondence with First Earl Canning 1846

105. Correspondence with Fifth Duke of Richmond 1846
     (NRA 7618 Canning)

NORTH AMERICA

Duke University, Williams R. Perkins Library
106. Letters to Sir John Newport 1816-1844, Guide 1900,
     p. 427. (NRA 29598 Newport)

Huntington Library, San Marino California
107. Letters to Grenville family. Guide to British MSS,1982

University of Michigan, William L. Clements Library
108. Miscellaneous Letters.
     Shy. MSS. in W.L. Clements Library, p. 15

Yale University Libraries, Beinecke Library
109. Letters to William Buckland 1836-1849
     (NRA 18661 Osborn Coll. - d61)

McGill University, McLennan Library
110.Letters to First Viscount Hardinge 1829-1848
     (NRA 7539 Hardinge)

CATALOGUES AND GUIDES

111. British Library
     Catalogue to Additions to Manuscripts in the British
     Museum (1836-)
     T.C. Skeat, The Catalogues of the Manuscript Collections
     (revised ed., 1970)
     British Library Journal (Spring 1975-)
     A twice-yearly periodical including information about
     new accessions (superseding British Museum Quarterly)

112. Public Record Office
     Guide to the Contents of the Public Record Office
     3 vols., 1963, 1968

113. Bodleian Library, Oxford
     F. Madan, H.H.E. Craster, N. Denholm-Young & R.W. Hunt,
     A Summary Catalogue of the Western Manuscripts in the
     Bodleian Library at Oxford (7 vols. in 8; only lists
      accessions to 1915)
     Bodleian Library Record
     Twice-yearly; includes notes on new accessions

114. Cambridge University Library
     A.E.B. Owen, A Summary Guide to the Accessions of
     Western Manuscripts (Other than Medieval) since 1867
     (1966). The Original Catalogue of the Manuscripts (5
     vols. & index) was published during 1856-1867.

115. National Library of Scotland
     Catalogue of Manuscripts (4 vols. published 1938-1971)
     Accessions of Manuscripts. Five Yearly; succeeded the
     Annual Report in 1959.

116. Scottish Record Office
     M. Livingstone, Guide to the Public Records of Scotland
     Deposited in H.M. General Register Office Edinburgh, 1905
     List of Gifts and Deposits in the Scottish Record Office
     (vol. I., 1971; vol. II., 1976)

17. India Office
     W. Foster, A Guide to the India Office Records 1600 -1858
     (1919, reprinted 1966)

118. Kent Archives Office
     F. Hull, Guide to the Kent County Archives Office 1958
     First Supplement 1971; Second Supplement 1981)
     Handlist of Kent County Records 1889-1945 (1972)

119. University College, London
     D.K. Coveney, Descriptive Catalogue of Manuscripts in
     the Library of University College, London (1935)
     Manuscript Collections in the Library, A Handlist
     (typescript, 1968)

120. Lambeth Palace Library
     E.G.W. Bill, Catalogue of Manuscripts (2 vols., 1972,
     1976)

121. Borthwick Institute of Historical Research, York
     University
     D.M. Smith, A Guide to the Archive Collections in the
     Borthwick Institute of Historical Research (1973, 1980

122. Philip Hepworth (ed.), Select Biographical Sources: The
     Library Association Manuscripts Survey (Library
     Association, 1971)

123. G.H. Martin & P. Spufford (eds.), The Records of the
     Nation 'Boydell Press, British Record Society, 1990)

124. Philip M. Hames (ed.), A Guide to the Archives and
     Manuscripts in the United States (Yale University
     Press, New Haven)

125. National Union Catalog of Manuscript Collections
     (Library of Congress, Washington, D.C)

THE HISTORICAL MANUSCRIPTS COMMISSION

The Royal Commission was established in 1869 for locating and
publishing manuscripts of institutions and private families. It
has published a number of Reports and Appendices, which contain
the summary descriptions of the archives of noble families,
individuals and ancient institutions and detailed calendars of
sections of these. The Commission did not, however, consider that
its activities extended into the nineteenth century, so its
publications are not relevant to the period of Peel.
     Nevertheless, the Commission is now publishing a series of
Guides to Sources for British History. Most useful for Peel

is this comprehensive reference-book:

126. Papers of British Politicians 1782-1900 (HMSO, 1989)

Also of value in this series is:

127. Guide to to the Location of Collections Described in the
     Reports and Calendar Series (HMSO, 1982)

Other relevant publications of the Commission are:

128. Manuscripts and Men (HMSO, 1969)
   A definitive illustrated catalogue for the Commission's
centenary year exhibition at the National Portrait Gallery,
London, in 1969.

129. J.D. Cantwell, The Public Record Office 1838-1958
     (HMSO, 1961)

130. Record Repositories in Great Britain (HMSO)
   The basic directory of repositories, which is revised
every few years.

131. Bulletin of the National Register of Archives
     (HMSO, 1848-1967)

132. Report of the Secretary to the Commissioners
     (HMSO, 1968-)

133. Accessions to the Repositories and Reports Added to the
     National Register of Archives (HMSO)
   Annual reports of major accessions received by the principal repositories in the year prior to publication.

2

Contemporary Newspapers and Journals

'The newspapers, Sir, they are the most villainous - licentious - abominable - infernal - Not that I ever read them - no, I make it a rule never to look into a newspaper,' declared Richard Brinsley Sheridan (1751-1816) in <u>The Critic</u>. Sheridan was not only a dramatist, but a politician as well. By the time of his death, however, it was impossible for a politician to adoopt such an attitude towards the press. There was a steady growth in the numbers and importance of newspapers during the first part of the nineteenth century. By 1815 there were 252 newspapers circulating in the United Kingdom, both national and provincial.

There were several reasons for this. One was a growing interest in public affairs, strongly stimulated by the political controversies of the time, which demanded accurate reports of parliamentary speeches and public events. The population of the country doubled between 1801 and 1851, particularly in the towns. The population of London grew from about 1,000,000 to about 2,400,000; and while in 1801 no provincial city had as many as 100,000 inhabitants, by 1851 seven had. And by then, for the first time in any country in the world, more people were living in towns than in the countryside. Moreover, the educational activities of both Anglicans and Nonconformists, together with a great working-class concern with politics, ensured that more of them were able and anxious to have access to news. The newspapers were thus presented with a greater and better situated readership.

There were also economic and technical developments which assisted the distribution of the newspapers. Between 1841 and 1846, the period of Peel's second administration, the railway mileage in the United Kingdom almost doubled from about 1,700 miles to over 3,000. Among other things, this made it possible for newsagents in London to send morning newspapers by an early mail to many parts of the country, and they reached Liverpool and Manchester by 2 p.m. Increasing trade brought greater revenue from advertisements, and the invention of steam printing after 1814 reduced costs and multiplied by nearly threefold to 1,100 the number of copies which could be printed in an hour. And the reduction of the newspaper duty in 1836 from 4d., to 1d. cut newspaper prices from 7d. to 4d. or 3d.

The press enjoyed greater freedom of expression as well. There was no preventive censorship; any action against newspapers only be taken after their publication.It has been estimated that between 1816 and 1834 there were 183 prosecutiions in Britain for seditious or blasphemous libel or defamation of the king and his ministers. Of these 131 took place in 1817 and between 1819 and 1821, and after 1824 the number was very small. Peel was largely responsible for this. When he became Home Secretary in 1822, he had come to realize that prosecution merely advertised an author and that it was difficult to obtain convictions, particularly in cases brought by the Constitutional Association, the Society for the Suppression of Vice and the Encouragement of Religion and Virtue throughout the United Kingdom and other organizations founded for this purpose.

Peel both criticized and valued the press. He criticized it because he feared that it was exerting an undue pressure upon governments and politicians in the name of representing public opinion. In 1820 he wrote about 'the tone of England - of that great compound of folly, weakness, prejudice, wrong feeling, right feeling, obstinancy and newspaper paragraphs, which is called public opinion.' At the same time, he realized the benefit exercised by the press in reporting the speeches of politicians, especially as public political meetings 1were not held in those days. 'My speech will, no doubt, be in the possession of everyone tomorrow morning,' he said in his first speech on the Corn Laws in 1846.' - Donald Read, _Peel and the Victorians_ (Basil Blackwell, Oxford, 1987), pp. 13, 36, 315.

134. R. Fox Bourne, _English Newspapers_ (2 vols., 1887)

135. W.D. Bowman, _The Story of the Times_ (Routledge, 1931)

136. Wilfrid Hindle, _The Morning Post_ (Routledge, 1931)

137. D. Hudson, _Thomas Barnes of the Times_ (CUP, 1943)

138. A. Aspinall, 'The Circulation of Newspapers in the Early Nineteenth Century,' _Review of English Studies_, vol. XXII (1946), pp. 29-43

139. A. Aspinall, _Politics and the Press c. 1780-1850_ (Home & Van Thal, 1949)

140. W.E. Andrews, _The British Newspapers_ (Basil Blackwell, Oxford, 1952)

141. R.K. Webb, 'Working Class Readers in Early Victorian England,' _English Historical Review_, vol. LXV (1950), pp. 333-351

142. E. Glasgow, 'The Establishment of the _Northern Star_ Newspaper,' _History_, vol. XXXIX (1954), pp. 28-35

143. A.P. Wadsworth, 'Newspaper Circulation 1800-1854,' _Transactions of the Manchester Statistical Society_ (1954-1955), pp. 386-401

144. R.K. Webb, The British Working Class Reader (1955)

145. R.K. Webb, 'The Victorian Reading Public,'
     Universities Quarterly, vol. XII, (1957)

146. Donald Read, 'North of England Newspapers (c. 1700 –
     c. 1900) and their Value to Historians,' Proceedings
     of the Leeds Philosophical Society, Literary and
     Historical Section, vol. VIII, (1957)

147. Donald Read, Press and People, 1790-1850 (Edward
     Arnold, 1961)

148. B. Ford (ed.), 'The Victorian Reading Public,' From
     Dickens to Hardy (1972)

149. Virginia Berridge, 'Popular Sunday Papers and Mid-
     Victorian Society,' G. Boyce et al.(eds.), Newspaper
     History (1978), ch. 13

150. Lists of Newspapers
     Cambridge Bibliography of English Literature (CUP,
     1940), vol. II, pp.720-730; vol. III, pp. 801-806

151. Daily News

A London newspaper established in 1842 as the organ of the new Liberalism (see no. 1061). From the start it championed the cause of free trade and the total repeal of the Corn Laws and so became a complete supporter of Peel. Its first editor was Charles Dickens, but he retired after 17 numbers and was replaced by John Forster, the historian historian and biographer. It was the first paper to be attached closely to the parliamentary Liberal party, but failed to gain popular support and its circulation by the the 1850's was not much beyond a thousand.

152. Leeds Mercury

A weekly newspaper established in 1718 and taken over in 1801 by Edward Baines, a supporter of the reform cause. He increased its circulation from about 800 copies a week in 1801 to about 10,000 in 1840, the largest circulation of any provincial newspaper. It came grudgingly to approve of Peel over the repeal of the Corn Laws and gave him a moderate measure of support.

153. Lloyd's Weekly Newspaper

A Sunday newpaper (with a first edition published on Friday afternoon for distribution from London to the provinces) founded in 1842 by Edward Lloyd (1815-1890) and read mainly by artisans and shopkeepers. At first hostile to Peel, in 1845 it considered that he had 'grown wiser.'

154. Manchester Courier

A Conservative weekly newspaper established in 1825. It was not an unqualified supporter of the Corn Laws, and in 1846 it praised Peel as a practical commercial statesman.

155. Manchester Guardian

A twice-weekly newspaper founded by middle-class reformers eighteen months after the 'Battle of Peterloo' (16th. August 1819) and described by Peel in 1839 as being 'read by every Whig and Dissenter in Lancashire' (D. Read, Peel and the Victorians, p. 72). It was critical of Peel until 1845 when it supported him wholly.

156. Morning Post

A Conservative daily newspaper established in 1772 to oppose the Morning Chronicle, a Whig paper established in 1769. It offered a formidable challenge to its rival and by 1803 had passed it in circulation. Staunchly protectionist, it became anti-Peel in 1845, while the Morning Chronicle, after becoming Palmerston's organ and containing anonymous articles by him, was bought by a group of Peelites in 1848.

157. Northern Star

A weekly newspaper started in Leeds in 1837 by the Chartist leader, Feargus O'Connor (1794-1855). Within a year it had a circulation of over 10,000 copies a week, more than any other provincial newspaper, its readership being entirely working-class. It consistently supported free trade, but never really trusted Peel. In the 1840's its circulation began to fall, and after being transferred to London in 1844, it came to an end in 1852.

158. Sheffield Independent

A weekly newspaper, which was founded in 1819 and became the organ of local middle-class reformers. It supported the Anti-Corn Law League and never became an admirer of Peel. By 1850 its circulation had reached 2,000, and it had done much to give Sheffield its reputation as an important mid-Victorian Radical centre.

159. Sheffield Mercury

A Conservative weekly newspaper established in 1807. It welcomed the Reform Bill of 1832, but thereafter became strongly opposed to the Whigs and upheld the protectionist cause. Its circulation rose to over 1,900 in 1836, the largest of any Sheffield newspaper, but in 1839 it was overtaken by the Sheffield Independent, and its sales fell steadily until it was absorbed in 1848 by the Sheffield Times, a new Peelite paper founded in 1846.

160. The Times

A daily London newspaper established in 1785. During Thomas

Barne's editorship (1817-1841), it became the leading London newspaper. It enjoyed the largest daily circulation, which quadrupled between 1837 and 1850 from about 10,000 to about 40,000 a day. Becoming independent of political subsidy, it ceased to support the government of the day and became instead the expression and guide of middle-class ideas. After some uncertainty, it supported the repeal of the Corn Laws though critical of Peel's handling of it.

161. Weekly Political Register

Founded in 1802 by William Cobbett (1762-1835), who has been called the 'father of modern journalism.' With one three months' break in 1817, it appeared with a circulation of between 60,000 and 100,000 copies a week until his death. Tory until 1804, it then became an expression of uncompromising and highly individualistic anti-establishment Radicalism urging with directness and vigour the need for governmental and social reform. It attacked Peel as an upholder of privilege and reaction. See also, Willian Cobbett, Cobbett's Legacy to Peel or an Inquiry with Respect to What the Right Honourable Baronet will do now with the House of Commons, with Ireland, with the English Church and the Dissenters, with the Swarms of Pensioners, etc., with the Crown Land and Army, with the Currency and the Debt (Cobbett's Register Office, 1835)

JOURNALS

Newspapers were not the sole means of giving expression to public opinion during the time of Peel. There were also periodicals and journals; and, indeed, these years saw important developments in such publications. While established titles, such as the Edinburgh Review and Quarterly Review were notably more serious and controversial, besides being longer and selling more widely than previous magazines and appealing especially to educated readers who were seriously concerned with politics and literature. The Illustrated London News and Punch were novel illustrated periodicals; and since Punch included political cartoons on its pages, it gave these a wider circulation than hitherto when they had only been sold separately by a few print-shops in London.

Information about nineteenth-century periodicals is elusive, but the University of Reading has an archive of this.

162. Annual Register

A yearly review giving a summary of the parliamentary history and main events of the previous year founded in 1758 by the writer and bookseller, Robert Dodsley, and still regularly published to-day. Like other reviews its not was political advocacy. During this period and particularly in the reign of William IV, its account of constitutional history displayed a considerable Tory outlook.

163. Blackwood's Edinburgh Magazine

A monthly magazine established in 1817 by a Scottish publisher, William Blackwood, to be a Tory rival in Edinburgh to the Edinburgh Review. It became famous for its scathing satire and violent attacks upon prominent personalities. It strongly criticized Peel in 1829 for his support of Roman Catholic Eamancipation, but moderated its attitude towards him personally, though retaining its support for protection.

164. Edinburgh Review and Critical Journal

A Whig quarterly founded in 1802 under the editorship of Francis Jeffrey, a Scottish advocate. With contributors such as Sydney Smith, Henry Brougham and Lord Macaulay, it soon attained a circulation of more than 10,000 copies. Though traditional in the world of literature, its politics were liberal, and it unhesitatingly supported the causes of parliamentary reform and free trade.

165. Gentleman's Magazine

Conducted by the London printer, Edward Cave, from 1731 to 1754 and published in altered formats until 1907. It provided entertaining writing by essayists, correspondents and poets together with political news, accounts of parliamentary debates, extracts from leading newspapers and pamphlets and original articles.

166. Illustrated London News

A weekly magazine established in 1842. Though few of its illustrations were taken from life, it attempted to depict important, transitory incidents, which was novel in contemporary journalism. It was cool towards Peel at first, but later considered him to be the most able and practical of the politicians of the time.

167. Punch or the London Charivari

A weekly magazine established in 1841 on the lines of the French satirical paper Charivari. Its success was largely due to its two talented cartoonists, John Leech (1817-1864), and Richard Doyle (1824-1883),who were considered to have drawn the most lifelike representations of Peel. And from being portrayed as a 'Knave of Spades' he became in 1845 a 'King of Hearts,' who sacrificed his political position in order to benefit the country by repealing the Corn Laws.

168. Quarterly Review

Established in 1809, largely through the influence of Sir Walter Scott, with the intention of being the Tory reply to the Edinburgh Review. Peel was closely in touch with it through his friend,J.W. Croker, who was its leading political writer. It reached a circulation of over 9,000 in 1841, but declined thereafter. It seems to have first popularized the name 'Conservative party.'

169. Westminster Review

Founded in 1824 by Radicals to answer both Tories and Whigs. It came to be quite favourable to Peel, whom it considered was displaying noticeable Radical aims in his policies.

3

Published Resources

Peel once said to a younger colleague, 'No public man who values
his character, ever destroys a letter or paper,' (John Morley,
Richard Cobden, p.391n.); and Gladstone told Archbishop Benson,
'The old Sir R. (Peel) preserved every letter written to him in so
perfect a way that Stanhope and others who were to write his life
could not face the mass of them, and the biography will never be
written.' - A.C. Benson, Edward White Benson, Archbishop of
Canterbury (Macmillan, 1901), p. 532.
    In fact, first Godwin Smith and then Edward Cardwell agreed to
write the official life of Peel, but both abandoned the project.
Stanhope did get as far as being the joint-editor of material
prepared by Peel (no. 194); and Parker, who had been Cardwell's
private secretary and later a Liberal Member of Parliament
produced Sir Robert Peel from his Private Papers (no. 200).
    Meanwhile, many papers about Peel were published during the
second half of the nineteenth century. These mainly reflected
the popular approval which he enjoyed during that time and also
tended to omit references to Queen Victoria and her personal
advisers which could have been painful or disrespectful to living
persons. Nor were there in the earlier years of this century very
many biographical and critical studies written upon him. This may
have been due to the reason given by Gladstone to the Archbishop,
but was more probably partly due to the inevitable reaction
against all things Victorian at this time, and also because the
material relevant to Peel, though voluminous, was not then as
readily available as was that at hand for some other leading
political figures.
    From the 1920's, however, attitudes changed, and scholarly
research into Peel was stimulated and given greater depth by the
deposit of the Peel papers in the British Museum (now the British
Library), the pioneer work in this direction being G. Kitson
Clark's political study (no. 206). Most recently there have
particularly been books and articles concerning the four areas of
policy - Roman Catholic Emancipation, Parliamentary Reform,
Ireland and the Corn Laws - upon which Peel changed his ideas, and
the consequences of his actions, especially for the Tory party
(e.g. nos.220, 224, 262, 266).

BIBLIOGRAPHIES

170. Lucy M. Brown & I.R. Christie (eds.), Bibliography of
     British History 1789-1914 (OUP, 1977)

171. H.J. Hanham (ed.), Bibliography of British History 1815-
     1914 (OUP,1976)

   Historical Association, Helps for Students of History -
172. I.R. Christie, British History Since 1760: A Select
     Bibliography (no. 12, 1970)
173. Owen Chadwick, The History of the Church: A Select
     Bibliography (no. 66, 1966)
174. E.M. Johnston, Irish History: A Select Bibliography
     (no. 73, 1972)

DOCUMENTARY COLLECTIONS

175. A. Aspinall & E.A. Smith (eds.), English Historical
     Documents, vol. XI, 1783-1832 (Eyre & Spottiswoode,
     1959)

176. G.M. Young & W.D. Hancock (eds.), English Historical
     Documents, vol. XII (I), 1833-1874 (Eyre & Spottiswoode,
1956)

177. Norman Gash (ed.), The Age of Peel (Documents of Modern
     History, Edward Arnold, 1968)

178. W.C. Costin & J.S. Warson (eds.), The Law and Working of
     the Constitution, vol. II, 1784 - 1914 (Adam & Charles
     Black, 1952)

179. H.J. Hanham, The Nineteenth-Century Constitution
     (CUP, 1969)

180. J.F.C. Harrison, Society and Politics in England
     1780-1960 (Harper & Row, New York, 1965)

181. G.D.H. Cole & A.W. Filson, British Working-Class
     Movements 1789-1875 (Macmillan, 1951)

182. R.P. Flindall, The Church of England 1815-1914
     (SPCK, 1972)
183. J. Briggs & I. Sellars, Victorian Nonconformity
     (Edward Arnold, 1972)

BIOGRAPHIES AND STUDIES

184. The Revd. Richard Davies, Memoirs of Sir Robert Peel
     (publ. anon., N.D.)
     A eulogy of the first Baronet; its authorship given by a
     copy in the Hawarden Library; published c. 1803-1804.

185. Anon., Sir Robert Peel and his Era (1843)
     A favourable account of Peel's achievements up to 1840.

186. Anon., Sir Robert Peel as Statesman and Orator (1846)

187. Sir Robert Peel and the Corn Law Crisis (2nd. ed., 1846)
A pamphlet published anonymously by Charles Greville (1794-1865), the political diarist.

188. H. Martin, A Personal Sketch of the Late Lamented Sir Robert Peel (Hamburg, 1850)

189. Von Heinrich Kunzel, Leben und Reden Sir Robert Peel's (2 vols., Hamburg, 1851)

190. G.H. Francis, The Late Sir Robert Peel, A Critical Biography (1852)

191. Thomas Doubleday, Life of Sir Robert Peel, An Analytical Biography (2 vols., 1856)

192. F.P.G. Guizot, Memoirs of Sir Robert Peel (Paris, 1857)
An account by a contemporary French historian and states-man, who himself knew Peel.

193. Sir Laurence Peel, A Sketch of the Life and Character of Sir Robert Peel (1860)
The author (1799-1884) was a cousin and contemporary of Sir Robert.

194. Earl Stanhope & E. Cardwell (eds.), Memoirs by the Rt. Hon. Sir Robert Peel (John Murray), 2 vols., 1865-1867)
Prepared by Peel himself and concerned mainly with Roman Catholic Emancipation, his first government and the repeal of the Corn Laws, illustrated with the assistance of both documents and explanations by Peel. Better edited than no. 200.

195. Henry Bulwer, Lord Dalling, Sir Robert Peel (1874)
The author was a diplomat, and the book is good on foreign policy.

196. G. Barnett Smith, Sir Robert Peel (English Political Leaders Series, 1881)

197. F.C.Montague, Life of Sir Robert Peel (Statesmen Series, W.H. Allen, 1888)

198. Justin McCarthy, Sir Robert Peel (Prime Ministers of Queen Victoria Series, Sampson Low, Marston, Searle & Rivington, 1891)
A tribute to Peel for his statesmanship.

199. J.R. Thursfield, Sir Robert Peel (Twelve English Statesmen Series, 1891)
An able development of the idea that Peel 'had insight, but not foresight.'

200. C.S. Parker (ed.), <u>Sir Robert Peel from his Private Papers</u> (John Murray, 3 vols., 1892-1899)
The most important published authority on Peel, being fuller than no. 194 and containing a comprehensive and important selection from most of the leading documents in no. 202, as well as several others (particularly to Henry Goulburn and to the Duke of Wellington) which are not there. It is, however, marred by altered words and phrases, unacknowledged omissions and conflations of letters of different dates. Much of the correspondence had already appeared in Wellington's <u>Despatches</u> (John Murray (1867-1880) and <u>The Croker Papers</u> (no. 285).

201. Lord Rosebery, <u>Sir Robert Peel</u> (Cassell, 1899)
A reprint from the <u>Anglo-Saxon Review</u> of a perceptive review of no. 200.

202. George Peel, <u>The Private Letters of Sir Robert Peel</u> (John Murray, 1920)
Mainly correspondence between Peel and his wife from no. 94.

203. H.W.C. Davis, <u>The Age of Grey and Peel</u> (OUP, 1929; reprinted 1964 & 1967)
A useful analysis of the parties and ideas of British politics during this period, which has stood the test of time.

204. A.A.W. Ramsay, <u>Sir Robert Peel</u> (Constable, 1828; reissued 1971)
The first scholarly biography of Peel based on manuscript sources. It is still particularly valuable for the period 1822-1832.

205. W.P. Morrell, <u>British Colonial Policy in the Age of Peel and Russell</u> (OUP, 1930)

206. G. Kitson Clark, <u>Sir Robert Peel and the Conservative Party: A Study in Party Politics, 1832-1841</u> (Bell, 1929; reprinted Frank Cass, 1964)
A long and detailed study, relying upon exact knowledge and careful research to consider how Peel recreated his party after the shattering events up to 1832 and faced its divided attachments to agriculture and industry.

207. G.Kitson Clark, <u>A Life of Peel</u> (Duckworth, 1936)
A short biography, but displaying some keen insights into Peel's personal character and political aims.

208. Tresham Lever, <u>The Life and Times of Sir Robert Peel</u> (Allen & Unwin, 1942)
Sets Peel's career against contemporary politics.

209. N. Vineis, <u>Robert Peel: La Ditatura del Libero Scambio</u> (O.E.T., Rome, 1946)
Represents Peel as a freedom-loving dictator.

210. Elie Halévy, The Age of Peel and Cobden (Benn,1947)
     Displays the accustomed intuition of this recognized
     expert on British nineteenth-century History.

211. G. Kitson Clark, The Life and Work of Sir Robert Peel:
     A Spoken Address in the New Technical College, Bury,
     on the 12th. December 1950 (Town Clerk's Department,
     Bury, Lancashire, 1951)

212. Norman Gash, Politics in the Age of Peel (Longmans,
     1953)
     A good account of the working of the political party
     system at this time.

213. T.L. Crosby, Sir Robert Peel's Administration, 1841-
     1846 (David & Charles, Newton Abbot, Devonshire, 1960)
     A condensed but well-proportioned and balanced account
     of this ministry.

214. Norman Gash, Reaction and Reconstruction in English
     Politics, 1832-1852 (OUP, 1965)
     Deals with the most important part of Peel's career
     and the rise of the Peelites.

215. Norman Gash, Mr. Secretary Peel (Longmans, 1961)
216. Norman Gash, Sir Robert Peel (Longmans,1972)
     A full and careful biography, the two volumes of which
     deal with Peel's career before and after 1830. It has
     unquestionably replaced all the previous lives of the
     statesman, though his generally favourable view of
     Peel has since met with some criticism in e.g. nos.
     223, 255, 267.

217. Robert Stewart, The Foundations of the Conservative
     Party, 1830-1867 (Longmans, 1978)
     Discusses Peel's public image and relations with his
     party and the effect his policies had upon its
     fortunes. See no. 221.

218. Norman Gash, Peel (Longmans,1976)
     An adapted, shortened and rewritten version of nos.
     215 and 216 without the acknowledgements, footnotes,
     references or bibliography which the earlier works
     possessed, but it has well-chosen illustrations not
     in the other volumes and a brief list of books and
     articles that are relevant.

219. Norman Gash, Aristocracy and People, Britain 1815-1865
     (The New History of England, vol. VIII, Edward Arnold,
     1979)
     Traces the stages by which the traditional governing
     classes, the landed aristocracy and gentry, adapted
     both themselves and the political system to the forces
     of rapid expansion and social change.

220. D.A. Kerr, Peel, Priests and Politics (OUP, 1982)
     Using fresh material,a valuable and impartial

study on the relationship between Peel's government of
1841-1846 and the Roman Catholic Church in Ireland.

221. Donald Read, <u>Peel and the Victorians</u> (Blackwell, Oxford,
1897)
Examine's Peel's popular reputation and his political and
social influence in Victorian times. A contrasting
analysis with no. 217.

222. P. Adelman, <u>Peel and the Conservative Party, 1830-1850</u>
(Seminar Studies, Longmans, 1989)
The effect that Peel's policies had upon his party during
those years together with the history of the Peelites
as they began the course that was to lead them to a
merger into the new Liberal party in 1859.

223. Eric J. Evans, <u>Sir Robert Peel, Statesmanship, Power and
Party</u> (Lancaster Pamphlets, Routledge, 1991)
A short study, asserting that Peel, rather than being
an excellent Prime Minister, brought about the break-up of
his party in 1846 and its decline into the wilderness.

224. <u>The Prime Ministers from Walpole to Macmillan</u>
(Dod's Parliamentary Companion, 1994)
A convenient factual guide.

ARTICLES AND ESSAYS

225. Walter Bagehot, 'The Character of Sir Robert Peel,'
<u>Biographical Studies</u> (Longmans, 1895)
A study of Peel by an influential economist and
journalist.

226. Sir S. Walpole, 'Sir Robert Peel,' <u>Studies in Biography</u>
(Fisher Unwin, 1907), pp. 9-48

227. W.E.H. Lecky, 'The Private Correspondence of Sir Robert
Peel,' <u>Historical and Political Essays</u> (Longmans, 1908),
pp. 151-199

228. Alfred Stern, 'A Letter of Sir Robert Peel Relative to
King Frederick William IV's Proposal to Summon the
Combined Diets, 1847,' <u>English Historical Review</u>, vol.
XXI (1913), pp. 542-546
The King of Prussia's decision to call together the
'United Diet' representing the various provinces of his
kingdom. See J. Haller, <u>The Epochs of German History</u>
(Routledge, 1930), p. 229.

229. R.L. Schluyer, 'British Imperial Preference and Sir
Robert Peel,' <u>Political Science Quarterly</u>, vol. XXXII
(1917), pp. 429-449

230. Ursilla N. MacDonnell, 'Sir Robert Peel: The Last
Phase,' <u>Queen's Quarterly</u>, vol. XXIX (1922), pp.
138-149

231. Sir R. Lodge, 'Sir Robert Peel,' F.J.C. Hearnshaw (ed.), Political Principles of Some Notable Prime Ministers of the Nineteenth Century (Macmillan, 1926), pp. 43-104.

232. Paul Knaplund, 'The Buller-Peel Correspondence Concerning Canada, 1841,' Canadian Historical Review, vol. VIII (1927), pp. 41-50

233. G.R.S. Taylor, 'Sir Robert Peel, 1788-1850,' Seven Nineteenth-Century Statesmen (Jonathan Cape, 1929), pp. 158-203

234. Henry Tristram, 'Catholic Emancipation: Mr. Peel and the University of Oxford,' Cornhill Magazine, vol. N.S. LXVI (1929), pp. 35-54

235. Paul Knaplund, 'Some Letters of Peel and Stanley on Canadian Problems, 1841-1844,' Canadian Historical Review, vol. XII (1931), pp. 45-54

236. R.C. Clark, 'Aberdeen and Peel in Oregon, 1844,' Oregon Historical Quarterly, vol. XXIV (1923), pp. 236-240

237. J.A. van Arkel, 'George Canning en Zijn Verhouding tot Sir Robert Peel,' Tijdschrift voor Geschiedenis, vol. L (1935), pp. 337-363
A consideration of the importance of Canning and Peel as statesmen.

238. Elie Halévy, 'Sir Robert Peel en 1841,' Révue Historique Moderne, vol.XII (Mars-Juin 1938), pp. 105-109
The problems facing Peel at the beginning of his ministry.

239. H.J. Laski, 'Robert Peel,' H.J. Massingham & Hugh Massingham (eds.), Great Victorians (Penguin Books, 1938), pp. 403-415

240. C.L. Cline, 'Disreali and Peel's 1841 Cabinet,' Journal of Modern History, vol. XI, no. 4 (December 1939), pp. 423-435
Why did Peel refuse to make Disraeli a minister?

241. Norman D. Palmer, 'Sir Robert Peel's "Select Irish Library,"' Irish Historical Studies, vol. VI, no. 22 (September 1948), pp. 101-113
Books collected by Peel when in Ireland.

242. J.W. Houseman, 'An Old Lithograph of Some Historical Importance: The Early Education of Sir Robert Peel,' Yorkshire Archaeological Journal , vol. XXVII, pt.145 (1848), pp. 72-79
A connection between Peel and Hipperholme Grammar School

243. R. Walker, 'Sir Robert Peel, Patron of the Arts,' Apollo, vol. LII (1950), pp. 16-18.

244. Norman Gash, 'Peel and the Party System, ' <u>Transactions of the Royal Historical Society</u>, Fifth Series, vol.I (1951), pp. 47-69

245. Asa Briggs, 'Sir Robert Peel,' <u>History Today</u>, vol.I (November 1951), pp. 25-31
Without Peel's reforms, 'there could have been no Golden Age of Victorian Britain.'

246. Asa Briggs, 'Sir Robert Peel,' Herbert van Thal (ed.), <u>British Prime Ministers</u> (2 vols., Allen & Unwin, 1953), vol. I, ch. 24

247. A.B. Cunningham, 'Peel, Aberdeen and the Entente Cordiale,' <u>Bulletin of the Institute of Historical Research</u>,' vol. XXX (1957), pp. 189-206,

248. Galen Broeker, 'Robert Peel and the Peace Preservation Force,' <u>Journal of Modern History</u> (December 1961)
Peel's pioneer establishment of a police force in Ireland.

249. J. Maudant Crook, 'Sir Robert Peel: Patron of the Arts,' <u>History Today</u>, vol. XVI (1966), pp. 3-11
A descriptive account of Peel's collection of paintings.

250. T.L. Fernandez, 'Sir Robert Peel, Nineteenth-Century Parliamentary Orator,' <u>Quarterly Journal of Speech</u>, vol. LII (1966), pp. 244-254

251. D.R. Fisher, 'The Opposition to Sir Robert Peel in the Conservative Party, 1841-1846.' (Unpublished Ph. D. thesis, Cambridge University, 1969.

252. D. Beales, 'Peel, Russell and Reform,' <u>Historical Journal</u> vol. XVII (1974), pp. 879-880

253. Norman Gash, 'Wellington and Peel,' Donald Southgate (ed.), <u>The Conservative Leadership,1832-1932</u> (Macmillan, 1974)

254. D.R. Fisher, 'Peel and the Conservative Party: The Sugar Crisis of 1844 Reconsidered, '<u>Historical Journal</u>, vol. XVIII (1975), pp. 279-302

255. Boyd Hilton, 'Peel: A Reappraisal,' <u>Historical Journal</u>, vol. XXII (1979), pp. 585-614
Peel was imnprisoned by his belief in free trade ideology, which weakened his wider political judgement.

256. G.I.T. Machin, 'Resistance to the Repeal of the Test and Corporation Acts, 1828,' <u>Historical Journal</u>, vol. XXII (1979), pp. 115-139

257. P.Marsh, 'The Conservative Conscience,' <u>The Conscience of the Victorian State</u> (Harvester Press, Hassocks, Sussex, 1979), pp. 215-242

258. R.W. Davis,' Toryism to Tamworth: The Triumph of Reform, ' Albion, vol. II (1980), pp. 922-931

259. D.A. Kerr, 'Peel and the Political Involvement of the Priests,' Archivium Hibernicum, vol. XXXVI (1931), pp. 16-25

260. Norman Gash, 'The Organization of the Conservative Party, 1832 - 1846. Part I: The Parliamentary Organization,' Parliamentary History, vol. I (1982 1983), pp. 137-165

261. Ian Newbould, 'Sir Robert Peel and the Conservative Party, 1832 - 1841: A Study in Failure?' English Historical Review, vol. CII (1983), pp. 529-557

262. David McIlwain, 'Sir Robert Peel,' John Canning (ed.), A Hundred Great Victorian Lives (Methuen, 1983), pp. 67-72

263. J. Seigel, 'Carlyle and Peel: The Prophet's Search for a Heroic Politician and an Unpublished Fragment,' Victorian Studies, vol. XXVI (1983), pp. 181-195

264. E. Jaggard, 'The 1841 British General Election: A Reconsideration,' Australian Journal of Politics and History, vol. XXX (1984), pp. 99-114

265. Gerard O'Brien, 'Robert Peel and the Pursuit of Catholic Emancipation, 1813 - 1817,' Archivium Hibernicum, vol. LVII (1988), pp. 141-155

266. Wendell V. Harris, 'Newman, Peel, Tamworth and the Concurrence of Historical Forces,' Victorian Studies, vol. XXXII (1989), pp. 187-208

267. David Eastwood, 'Peel and the Tory Party Reconsidered,' History ToDay, vol. XXXII (March 1992), pp. 27-33 Peel believed parliament could dispense with parties.

268. A.J.P. Taylor, 'Orange Peel' and 'The Cotton Spinner's Son,' Europe from Napoleon to the Second International, Essays on the Nineteenth Century, ed. Chris Wrigley (Hamish Hamilton, 1993), pp. 120-128

MEMOIRS, DIARIES AND LETTERS

269. The Aberdeen-Lieven Correspondence, 1832-1845, ed. E. Jones Parry (Camden Third Series, vol. LX, LXII, 1926, 1928)

270. Correspondence of Charles Arbuthnot, ed. A. Aspinall, (Camden Third Series,vol. LIX, 1937)

271. Journal of Mrs. Arbuthnot, 1820-1832 ed. F. Bamford & the Duke of Wellington (2 vols., Macmillan, 1950)

272. A Aspinall (ed.), <u>Three Early Nineteenth-Century Diaries</u>
(Williams & Norgate, 1952)
The diarists are: Sir Denis Le Marchant; Earl
Ellenborough; Edward John Littleton.

273. <u>Beaconsfield Letters: Lord Beaconsfield's Letters, 1830-
1852</u>, ed. R. Disraeli (John Murray, 1887)

274. Benjamin Disraeli, Lord Beaconsfield, <u>Life of Lord
George Bentinck</u> (Colburn, 1851)

275. Lord Broughton, <u>Recollections of a Long Life</u>, ed. Lady
Dorchester (4 vols., 1910)

276. Duke of Buckingham, <u>Memoirs of the Court of George IV</u>
(2 vols., 1859)

277. <u>Memoirs of Baron Bunsen</u>, ed. F. von Bunsen (Longmans,
2 vols., 1868)

278. T. Moore, <u>Life and Letters of Byron</u> (John Murray,
1908)

279. Sir H.E. Maxwell, <u>Life and Letters of the Fourth Earl
of Clarendon</u> (Edward Arnold, 2 vols., 1913)

280. W.J. Patrick (ed.), <u>Recollections of Lord Cloncurry</u>
(Dublin, 1855)

281. <u>Diary and Correspondence of Charles Abbot, Lord
Colchester</u>, ed. Lord Colchester (3 vols., 1861)

282. Hon. George Pellew, <u>Life and Correspondence of Henry
Addington, Viscount Sidmouth</u> (3 vols., 1861)

283. <u>Creevey's Life and Times</u>, ed. John Gore (John Murray,
1934)

284. <u>The Creevey Papers</u>, ed. Sir H. Maxwell (John Murray,
1903)

285. <u>Correspondence and Diaries of J.W. Croker</u>, ed. L.J.
Jennings (John Murray, 3 vols., 1884)

286. <u>The Croker Papers, 1808-1857</u>, ed. Bernard Pool
(Batsford, 1957)

287. <u>Letters of the First Earl of Dudley to the Bishop
of Llandaff</u> (1841)

288. <u>Dyott's Diary</u>, ed. R.W.Jefferey (Archibald Constable,
2 vols., 1907)

289. <u>The Diary of Henry Hobhouse, 1820-1827</u>, ed. Arthur
Aspinall (Home & Van Thal, 1947)

290. Abraham. D. Kriegel, The Holland House Diaries, 1830-1840 (Routledge, 1977)

291. Political Diary of Edward Law, Lord Ellenborough, ed. Lord Colchester (2 vols., Bentley, 1907)

292. Carola Oman, The Gascoyne Heiress, The Life and Diaries of Frances Mary Gascoyne Cecil, 1802-1839 (Hodder & Stoughton, 1968)

293. The Letters of King George IV, 1812-1830, ed. A. Aspinall (3 vols., CUP, 1938)

294. The Gladstone Diaries, ed. M.R.D. Foot & H.C.G. Matthew (OUP, 1974)

295. C.S. Parker, Life and Letters of Sir James Graham (2 vols., John Murray, 1907)

296. Mr. Gregory's Letter-Box, ed. Lady Gregory (1898)

297. The Greville Memoirs, 1817-1860, ed. Henry Reeve (8 vols., Longmans, Green, 1875-1887); ed. Lytton Strachey & Roger Fulford (8 vols., Macmillan, 1938; ed. Roger Fulford (1 vol., Batsford, 1963)
Since these several editions are in use, the common practice (which is followed here) is to give references to dates rather than to volumes and pages.

298. Gervase Huxley, Lady Elizabeth and the Grosvenors, Life in a Whig Family, 1822-1839 (OUP, 1965)

299. Memories of Anna Maria Wilhelmina Pickering, ed. Spencer Pickering (Hodder & Stoughton, 1933)

300. Diary of B.R. Haydon, ed. W.H. Pope (5 vols., Harvard, 1960-1963

301. Lord Stanmore, Sidney Herbert, A Memoir (2 vols., Methuen, 1906)

302. Memoir of J.C. Herries, ed. E. Herries (2 vols., John Murray, 1880)

303. The Huskisson Papers, ed. Louis Melville (Constable, 1931

304. The Lieven- Palmerston Correspondence, 1828-1856, trans. & ed. Lord Dudley (John Murray, 1943)

305. Thomas Raikes, Journal, 1831-1847 (Longmans, Green, 3 vols., 1856-1857)

306. O. Williams, Life and Letters of John Rickman (Constable, 1912)

307. J.G. Lockhart, <u>Memoirs of the Life of Sir Walter Scott</u>
(10 vols., Edinburgh, 1839)

308. W. Torrens McCullagh, <u>Memoirs of the Rt. Hon. R.L. Sheil</u>
(2 vols., 1855)

309. <u>Diary of Philipp Neumann</u> (trans. & ed. E. Beresford
Chancellor (2 vols., Allan, 1928)

310. T. Wemyss Reid, <u>Memoirs and Correspondence of Lyon
Playfair</u> (Cassell, 1899)

311. <u>Diary of Frances Lady Shelley, 1787-1861</u>, ed. R.
Edgcumbe (2 vols., John Murray, 1912-1913)

312. <u>The Letters of Queen Victoria, 1837-1861</u>, ed. A.C.
Benson & Viscount Esher (3 vols., John Murray, 1908)

313. <u>Memoirs of Robert Plumer Ward</u>, ed. E. Phipps (2 vols.,
1850)

4

Parliamentary Papers and Debates

The most important parliamentary papers concerning Peel are the published reports of the following Committees of the House of Commons:

314. 1810 II   Cash Payments
315. 1816 III   Children in the Manufactories
316. 1816 IV   Police of the Metropolis
317. 1822 V   Police of the Metropolis
318. 1828 VI   Police of the Metropolis
319. 1839 XIX   County Constabulary

Two guides to the printed resources reporting the debates in the House of Commons are:

320. John A. Woods, A Bibliography of Parliamentary Debates of Great Britain (House of Commons Library Document, No. 2, HMSO, 1956)

321. David Lewis Jones, Debates and Proceedings of the British Parliaments (House of Commons Library Document No. 16, HMSO, 1986)

Not until 1909, when the government took over the publication of Hansard as the official record, have there been strictly verbatim reports of parliamentary debates. For Peel's period the published sources are:

322. W. Cobbett, The Parliamentary History of England, from the Earliest Period to the Year 1803

323. T.C. Hansard, Parliamentary Debates from 1803

324. A. Aspinall, 'The Reporting and Publishing of the House of Commons' Debates, 1771-1834,' Essays Presented to Sir Lewis Namier (Macmillan, 1956)

Peel's speeches in Parliament sre collected in:

325. The Speeches of the late Right Honourable Sir Robert Peel in the House of Commons (4 vols., 1853)
This is not complete, but it is extensive and contains a good index and chronological summary.

5

Contemporaries of Peel

LORD ABERDEEN (1784-1860)

Lady Peel wrote to Lord Aberdeen a month after her husband's
death, 'My beloved always talked to you as the friend whom he most
valued, for whom he had the sincerest affection, whom he esteemed
higher than any.' (CSP, vol., III, p. 555). George Hamilton
Gordon, Fourth Earl of Aberdeen, was educated at Harrow and
Cambridge and, after occupying diplomatic posts, served in
Peel's ministries as Secretary for War and Colonies (1833-1835)
and Foreign Secretary (1841-1846). He shared Peel's wish for a
pacific foreign policy, to whom his diplomatic experience was
invaluable. Together they were particularly successful in their
relationship with France, though Peel took a firmer attitude
towards Louis Philippe's foreign adventures than he did. He
supported Peel over the repeal of the Corn Laws, followed him out
of office and became the Peelite leader after his death. Two
years later he led a Whig-Peelite administration, but in the
Crimean War he missed the support of Peel's drive and resolution
and resigned in 1855.

326. Lord Stanmore, The Earl of Aberdeen (Sampson Low, 1893)

327. Lady Frances Balfour, The Life of George, Fourth Earl of
     Aberdeen (Hodder & Stoughton, 2 vols., 1922)

328. Muriel E. Chamberlain, Lord Aberdeen (Longmans, 1983)

GEORGE CANNING (1770-1827)

Still more than Peel, Canning belonged to a new class of
politicians. His mother was an actress, and he was rescued from
poverty and educated at Eton and Oxford by relatives. He entered
Parliament in 1794 as a supporter of the Younger Pitt. He was
Foreign Secretary from 1807 to 1809 during a critical period of
the Napoleonic War, and his seizure of the Danish and Portuguese
fleets, to save them from French control, probably preserved
England from invasion by Napoleon; but his lowly social origins,
combined with his acid wit and clear ambition, prejudiced the
party magnates against him, and he lacked office for many years.
When he again was Foreign Secretary in 1822, he firmly supported
Greek and South American independence and brought about the

promulgation of the Monroe Doctrine in 1823 to prevent any 'future colonization by European powers' in the continent of America and secured its enforcement with the support of the British navy. In his own words he called 'the new world into existence to redress the balance of the old.'

As a disciple of Pitt, he was a liberal-minded Tory and favoured Roman Catholic Emancipation, which brought him into conflict with Peel. This began in 1817 when Peel was elected one of the burgesses in Parliament for Oxford University, a position which Canning wanted.(se no. 000) and culminated with Peel's refusal to serve under him during his brief period of Prime Minister in 1827.

329. H. Temperley, George Canning (1907)

330. H. Temperley, The Foreign Policy of Canning, 1822-1827 (Bell, 1925)

331. A. Aspinall, 'The Canningite Party,' Transactions of the Royal Historical Society, vol. XXXII (1982),p. 27

333. Sir Charles Petrie, George Canning (Eyre & Spottiswoode, 2nd. ed., 1946)

334. Peter Dixon, Canning, Politician and Statesman (Weidenfeld & Nicolson, 1976)

RICHARD COBDEN (1804-1865)

Cobden is commonly associated in his active opposition to the Corn Laws with the name of John Bright (1811-1865), but Cobden was, in fact, the more important of the two men.He was the mastermind behind the successful activities of the Anti- Corn Law League, while Bright, despite the moving force of his parliamentary oratory was a follower rather than a leader. It was with Cobden and not Bright that Peel came into contact with the events that led him to undertake the repeal.

Cobden was the son of a small south-country farmer and set himself up as a textile manufacturer in Manchester, where he took part in municipal politics and became associated with the Anti-Corn Law League. Its leaders used very violent language hich alarmed the government (see no. 1040); and Cobden attacked Peel personally at its meetings, but when in 1843 (less than a month after the assassination of Peel's private secretary), he wildly criticized Peel Peel in the House of Commons (see no. 998), there was an uproar. He apologized, but resented the sharp retort Peel had made to him. He continued to use strong language about Peel until a reconciliation was effected between the two men in 1846 (see no. 000). Peel had forgotten about the incident but Cobden resented it until Peel placated him.

By then Peel had become convinced by Cobden of the vital need to repeal the Corn Laws (see no. 1026); and when, after carrying this into effect, he was defeated in Parliament, he paid a warm tribute in his resignation speech to Cobden's leading part in securing the repeal (see no. 1098). Concentration upon the campaign had led Cobden to neglect his business interests.

Grateful manufacturers subscribed for him a sum of £76,760, which enabled him to buy his birthplace at Dunford, near Midhurst in Sussex, and rebuild it in the style suitable for a country gentleman.

335. Sir Louis Mallet, The Political opinions of Richard Cobden (Macmillan, 1869)

336. Henry Ashworth, Recollections of Richard Cobden M.P. and the Anti-Corn Law League (Cassell, Petter & Galpin, 1877)

337. John Morley, The Life of Richard Cobden (Fisher Unwin, 1903; American Edition, Roberts Brothers, Boston)

338. Elie Halévy, The Age of Cobden and Peel, A History of the English People, 1841-1852 (Benn, 1947)

339. Asa Briggs, 'Cobden and Bright,' History Today, vol. VII (August 1957),pp. 495-503

340. Donald Read, Cobden and Bright, A Victorian Political Partnership (Edward Arnold, 1967)

341. J.Prest, Politics in the Age of Cobden (Macmillan, 1977)

342. Wendy Hinde, Richard Cobden, A Victorian Outsider (Yale University Press, New Haven, 1987)

BENJAMIN DISRAELI (1804-1881)

The strangest prominent figure in British politics during the nineteenth century was Benjamin Disraeli, who was made Earl of Beaconsfield in 1876. His father was a cultivated man of letters, who broke away from Judaism and had his children baptized, which relieved them of the political restrictions then imposed upon Jews. Having supported himself by writing, he entered Parliament as a Tory in 1837 and married a wealthy widow two years later. His maiden speech in the House of Commons was disastrous, his oriental appearance, dandyfied attire and affected manner gaining him a hostile reception. He shouted above the jeering, 'I will sit down now, but the time will come when you will hear me!'

As the days of the Whig government were by now clearly drawing to an end, Disraeli was anxious to stand well with Peel and in 1841,though he had not yet achieved political prominence, he asked him for an appointment and was bitterly disappointed when he did not succeed. Believing that he could not hope for promotion under Peel, he put himself at the head of a growing number of Tories who were opposed to his free trade policy and launched a series of scathing and telling attacks upon him. The climax came when, on the same day as the passing of the Corn Law Bill, he secured the defeat of Peel and turned him out of office forever.

The result was calamitous for the Tories and not immediately beneficial for Disraeli. Nearly all the talented members of the party were Peelites, and Lord Stanley (later fourteenth Earl of Derby) was now the acknowledged leader of the Tories in the House

of Commons. Disraeli did not gain this position until the winter
of 1851-1852, but he then set out to form a new Conservative party
with an emphasis on social legislation(as Peel would have
wished) combined with a popular imperial policy.

343. W.F. Monypenny & G.E. Buckle, The Life of Benjamin
     Disraeli, Earl of Beaconsfield (6 vols., John Murray,
     1910-1922

344. B.R. German, The Young Disraeli (Bell, 1960)

345. Robert Blake, 'The Young Disraeli,' H.R. Trevor Roper
     (ed.), Essays in British History Presented to Sir Keith
     Feiling (Macmillan, 1964)

346. E.J. Feuchtwanger, Disraeli, Democracy and the Tory
     Tory Party (OUP, 1968)

347. Robert Blake, Disraeli (Methuen, 1969)

348. Sarah Bradford, Disraeli (Weidenfeld & Nicolson, 1982)

349. Stanley Weintraub, Disraeli, A Biography (Hamish
     Hamilton, 1993)

WILLIAM EWART GLADSTONE (1809-1898)

Like Peel himself, Gladstone came from the classes enriched by
the Industrial Revolution. From humble origins, his father
became a wealthy Liverpool merchant. He had his son educated at
Eton and at Christ Church, Oxford, the same college as Peel, and
where he also obtained a double first in 1831. He had already
shown in Oxford the intense religious feeling, which was to last
all his life, and he thought at first of seeking ordination in the
Church of England. His father, however, had the same ambition for
him as did Peel's, and he did as his father wished. He accepted
the seat offered to him by the Duke of Newcastle and entered
Parliament as a Tory member for the borough of Newark in
Nottinghamshire in 1832.
    He drew attention to himself in his first speech in 1833, in
which he favoured the 'gradual emancipation' of slaves, and in
1834 Peel made him Junior Lord of the Treasury and the next year
Under-Secretary for War and Colonies in his first short-lived
government. While in opposition Gladstone wrote The State in
Relation with the Church in 1838 and Church Principles
Considered in their Results in 1840, which upheld the dominant
position of the Church of England in the constitution. Peel's
comment upon them was, 'That young man will ruin a fine career if
he writes such books as these!'
    He had, however, a career before him when 'his reputation was
made in the field of finance, to which, under Sir Robert Peel's
guidance, he graduated directly from that of theology'
(Philip Magnus, Gladstone, p. xi). His entry into financial
affairs came with Peel's second government. Peel made him Vice-
President of the Board of Trade in 1841 and President of the
Board of Trade with a seat in the Cabinet the next year. When the
government embarked in 1842 upon the policy of freeing trade and
making good the loss of revenue by reviving the income tax which
Pitt had formerly imposed as a wartime measure, Gladstone

undertook the greater amount of the work and exhibited his grasp of financial detail for which he was praised by Peel.

While engaged in the second revision of the tariff system in 1845, Gladstone resigned from his office because he disapproved of the grant to Maynooth College. His acceptance of Peel's decision to repeal the Corn Laws led him to becoming Secretary of State for the Colonies in 1845, but he had to follow Peel out of office the next year. He supported Peel when he made his last speech in 1850 in opposition to Palmerston's Greek policy. After Peel's death he remained a Peelite until moving into the Liberal party.

350. John Morley, <u>Life of Gladstone</u> (2 vols., Edward
     Lloyd,1908)

351. F.W. Hirst, <u>Gladstone as Financier and Economist</u> (Methuen,
     1931)

352. F.E. Hyde, <u>Gladstone at the Board of Trade</u> (Cobden-
     Sanderson, 1934)

353. J.L. Hammond & M.R.D. Foot, <u>Gladstone and Liberalism</u>
     (English Universities Press, 1932)

354. Philip Magnus, <u>Gladstone</u> (John Murray, 1963)

355. E.G. Collieu, <u>Gladstone</u> (OUP,1968)

356. M.R.D. Foot & H.C.G. Matthew (eds.), <u>The Gladstone
     Diaries</u> (OUP,1974, vol. III)

357. H.C.G. Matthew, <u>Gladstone 1809-1874</u> (OUP, 1986)

SIR JAMES GRAHAM (1792-1861)

Entering Parliament as a Whig in 1826, Graham supported Roman Catholic Emancipation and the Reform Bill. Earl Grey made him First Lord of the Admiralty, in 1830, but he resigned in 1834 over the government's plan to suppress ten Irish bishoprics (which led to the Tractarian movement in the Church of England) and lost his seat the next year. A sympathetic letter to him from Peel brought a reply (no. 898) which resulted in a close friendship between them. He returned to Parliament in 1838, and Peel made him Home Secretary in 1841. He dealt ably with the trial of O'Connell (see no. 1017) and warmly supported the repeal of the Corn Laws. The defeat of his bill for the protection of life in Ireland in 1846 brought about the fall of the ministry. He resigned from office and was subsequently active with the Peelites. When Peel was dying,he asked for Graham, who was there to the end.

358. C.S. Parker, <u>Life and Letters of Sir James Graham</u>
     (2 vols.,John Murray, 1907)

359. J.T. Ward, <u>Sir James Graham</u> (Macmillan,1967)

WILLIAM HUSKISSON (1770-1830)

Among the spectators watching the storming by the mob of the fortress-prison in Paris, the Bastille, in July 1789, the event which began the French Revolution, was a young Englishman, William Huskisson. Owing to the financial difficulties of his father, a Worcestershire squire, he was educated in Paris by a great-uncle. On his return to England, he became a Tory M.P. in 1796, but the effect of his time in France always made him more liberal in his outlook than most of the members of the party. After holding several minor offices, he became President of the Board of Trade in 1823 and in 1827 Colonial Secretary. During that time he began the move towards free trade, which Peel later pursued, by reducing import duties and removing restrictions on trade with the colonies. Huskisson's liberal attitude towards parliamentary reform compelled him to resign from Wellington's government in 1828. While attending the ceremonial opening of the Liverpool and Manchester Railway in September 1830, he was accidentally killed when he fell before a locomotive engine.

360. Life and Speeches of William Huskisson (3 vols., 1831)

LORD LIVERPOOL (1770-1828)

Robert Banks Jenkinson, who was created Baron Hawkesbury in 1803 and succeeded as second Earl of Liverpool in 1808, was educated at the Charterhouse and Christ Church, Oxford and entered Parliament as a Tory in 1790. Having served in previous ministries as Foreign Secretary (when he negotiated the unpopular Treaty of Amiens in 1802) and Home Secretary, he was made Secretary of State for War and the Colonies by Spencer Perceval in 1809, and he appointed Peel, whose performance in the House of Commons had impressed him, as his Under-Secretary. When Perceval was assassinated in 1812, Liverpool became Prime Minister and formed an administration which lasted foe nearly fifteen years. He chose Peel as Secretary for Ireland, though he admitted that it was because he was short of good men for his administration (see. no. 709).

These were the years when victory over France was achieved and was followed by the period of political and social unrest caused by the post-war slump in trade and manufacture, industrialization, over-populatiion and urban growth. The government countered this with the repressive Six Acts of 1819, which Peel, who had resigned his post in 1818, supported as necessary to safeguard order and property in the country.

In 1822, however, as trade improved and discontent died down, Liverpool reconstructed his Cabinet and embarked upon a policy of 'liberal Toryism,' which he had intended to adopt for some time. Among his new appointments was that of Peel as Home Secretary, whose wide-ranging reforms of the criminal law and the prison system received his full support. He was able to forward the policy of the government by his ability to get its strong-minded and discordant members to work together. He succeeded in uniting the old and new Tories at a critical period. His unique skill in doing this was shown when his resignation in 1827, after being struck with apoplexy, was followed by the disintegration of unity in the Cabinet.

361. C.D. Yonge, The Life of Robert Banks Jenkinson, Second Earl of Liverpool (3 vols., Macmillan, 1868)

362. W.R. Brock, Lord Liverpool and Liberal Toryism, 1820-1827 (CUP, 1941; reissued Cassell, 1967)

363. Sir Charles Petrie, Lord Liverpool and his Times James Barrie, 1954)

364. Norman Gash, 'The Earl of Liverpool,' Herbert van Thal (ed.), The Prime Ministers (Allen & Unwin, 2 vols.,1974)

365. Norman Gash, Lord Liverpool (Weidenfeld & Nicolson, 1984)

LORD MELBOURNE (1779-1848)

William Lamb, second Viscount Melbourne, came of a wealthy legal family and was educated at Eton and Trinity College, Cambridge. He entered the House of Commons as a Whig in 1806, but lost his seat in 1812 and was not re-elected until 1812. He was attracted by Canning's 'liberal Toryism' and served under him as Chief Secretary for Ireland in 1827. He held the same post under Wellington in 1828, but resigned with other Canningites later that year. In the next year his father's death removed him to the House of Lords, where he reverted to his Whig principles. In 1830 he became Home Secretary under Lord Grey, whom he succeeded as Prime Minister in 1834. He performed the valuable task of training the young Queen Victoria in her regal duties, but this resulted in the 'Bedchamber Incident' of 1839 (see nos. 910-928). He finally had to resign from the premiership when Peel secured the passing of a vote of no-confidence against his government in 1841. He was very much an eighteenth-century figure, fastidious and politically indolent. He married Lady Caroline Ponsonby in 1805,but her affair with Lord Byron resulted in their formal separation in 1825. He was subsequently involved in two divorce cases.

366. Henry Dunckley, Lord Melbourne (Sampson, Low, 1880)

367. Lord David Cecil, The Young Melbourne (Pan Books,1938)

368. Lord David Cecil, Lord M (Arrow Books, 1962)

DANIEL O'CONNELL (1775-1847)

Descended from an English settler in Ireland in Elizabethan times, O'Connell was educated in France for the Roman Catholic priesthood, but then trained as a lawyer in London. He became famous as a counsel in Ireland and had a profitable practice. Drawn increasingly into politics, he soon became accepted as the virtual leader of the campaign for Roman Catholic Emancipation. This brought him into conflict with Peel, whom he unsuccessfully challenged to a duel in 1815 (see. nos. 731-738), which resulted in a lifelong personal hostility between the two men.

His foundation of the Catholic Association in 1823, supported by his outstanding organizing ability and powerful oratory, and his election to Parliament for County Clare in 1828 were largely responsible for Peel's acceptance of Roman Catholic Emancipation (see nos. 801-811). He went on to campaign for the repeal of the Act of Union, again holding many 'monster meetings' all over Ireland, for which Peel in 1843 had him imprisoned for sedition, but he was released on appeal to the House of Lords. By then, however, the Irish famine had overshadowed this constitutional issue, and his political influence declined.

369. Sean O'Faolian, King of the Beggars (Nelson,1938)

370. Angus Macintyre, The Liberator (Hamish Hamilton, 1965)

371. K.B. Nowlan, The Politics of Repeal (Routledge,1965)

LORD PALMERSTON (1784-1865)

Henry John Temple, third Viscount Palmerston, was educated at Harrow, Edinburgh University and Cambridge. He succeeded to his father's title in 1802, and as this was an Irish peerage he was able to enter the House of Commons in 1807 as a Tory. The question of parliamentary reform brought him into the Whig party. Grey made him Foreign Secretary in 1830, and he held that position (except during Peel's brief administration) until 1841. During that time he asserted his vigorous self-confidence in the interest of both the cause of nationalism and British interests. He was prominent in securing Belgian independence in 1830, in forming the Quadruple Alliance of 1834 against the pretenders to the Spanish and Portuguese thrones and in supporting Turkey first against Russian and then Egyptian encroachment.

He became Foreign Secretary again in 1846. Peel's last speech in the House of Commons, on the day before his fatal accident, was in the affair of Don Pacifico, a Gibraltar Jew living in Athens, whom Palmerston forcefully supported as a British subject in a dispute with the Greek government. He condemned Palmerston for using diplomacy 'to fester every wound, to provoke instead of soothing resentments.' The policy of 'Pam,' however, was very popular with contemporary British public opinion.

372. Kingsley Martin, The Triumph of Lord Palmerston
     (Hutchinson,1936)

373. Donald Southgate, The Most English Minister: The
     Policies and Politics of Palmerston (Macmillan,
     (1966)

374. Jasper Ridley, Lord Palmerston (Constable, 1970)

QUEEN VICTORIA (1819-1901) AND PRINCE ALBERT (1819-1861)

When the young Queen Victoria came to the throne in 1837, Lord Melbourne was the Prime Minister of a Whig government. She immediately became attached to him, not really for political reasons, but rather because she was personally attracted to him by his charming, fatherly attitude towards her. She was dismayed when his government's defeat led to his resignation in 1839.

She sent for Peel to ask him to form a government and did

907). She was displeased by his awkward, nervous manner, Lancashire accent and unsuccessful efforts to be at ease with her. There followed the Bedchamber Crisis (see nos. 910-928), which resulted in the return of Melbourne to power again until 1841 when his defeat this time unavoidably brought Peel back into office.

Victoria still disliked Peel and persisted in maintaining a secret correspondence with Melbourne, which might have caused another constitutional crisis had not Melbourne been incapacitated by a stroke at the end of 1842. And by then her hostility towards Peel had disappeared. He was now her 'dear Sir Robert,' whose conversation, as he unfroze, she found 'very interesting.'

Her change of attitude towards him was encouraged by Prince Albert, whom she married in 1840. Peel and the Prince admired and trusted each other as believers in efficiient pragmatism in public administration. And Albert saw Peel as linked with the industrial classes, whom he approved, rather than with the aristocracy, the 'fashionables' and 'fox-hunters,' whose support he found difficult to secure when he arrived in the country.

In February 1842 Peel indicated that he would keep the Prince informed about the intentions of the government (see no. 966); and from the time when Victoria gave birth to the Prince of Wales in November 1842, Peel began to give him nightly reports of the debates in the House of Commons and summaries of the discussions in the Cabinet. From that year too the Prince attended the audiences which ministers had with the Queen. Peel recognized also that they shared common artistic interests and in 1841 placed him at the head of the Royal Commission on the rebuilding of the Houses of Parliament. After Peel's death, Albert took the unusual step, as a member of the royal family, of paying a public tribute in a speech (no. 1132).

Peel's appreciation of Victoria's beloved husband increased her affection for him, as also did the help he gave them in buying Osborne House (see no. 1007). For the rest of his career, he received royal approval for all that he did. She admired him as a dedicated leader, who put the good of her kingdom above all considerations of party politics. A few hours after his death, she wrote in her Journal, 'Belonging to no party, he stood as the first name in the House of Commons.' Still influenced by Melbourne's Whiggery, she believed that he really shared its outlook and wrote later, 'It was poor Sir Robert's misfortune to have been kept down to old Tory principles, for which his mind was far too enlightened.' (Royal Archives, Windsor Castle).

375. Arthur Ponsonby (Lord Ponsonby of Shulbrede), Queen Victoria (Duckworth, 1933)

376. Roger Fulford, Queen Victoria (Collins, 1951)

377. D. Creston, The Youthful Queen Victoria (Macmillan, 1952)

378. A. Cecil, Queen Victoria and her Prime Ministers (Eyre & Spottiswoode, 1953)

379. Elizabeth Longford, <u>Victoria R.I.</u> (Weidenfeld &
     Nicolson, 1964); published in USA as <u>Queen Victoria,
     Born to Succeed</u> (Harper & Row, New York, 1965)

380. Alison Plowden, <u>The Young Victoria</u> (Weidenfeld &
     Nicolson, 1981)

381. Stanley Weintraub, <u>Victoria, Biography of a Queen</u>
     (Unwin Hyman, 1987; Trumn Valley Books,USA)

     *   *   *   *   *

382. Sir Theodore Martin, <u>The Life of H.R.H. the Prince
     Consort</u> (5 vils.,1878-1880)

383. Roger Fulford, <u>The Prince Consort</u> (Macmillan, 1949)

384. Frank Eyck, <u>The Prince Consort, A Political Biography</u>
     (Chatto & Windus, 1959)

DUKE OF WELLINGTON (1769-1852)

Arthur Wellesley was created Viscount Wellington in 1809, Earl
and Marquis of Wellington in 1812 and Duke of Wellington in 1814.
After the culmination of his active military service at the
Battle of Waterloo in 1815, he commanded the British army of
occupation in France until his return to England in 1818, when he
took his place in the House of Lords as a Tory strongly supporting
aristocratic government and opposed to Roman Catholic
Emancipation.
     He served in Liverpool's government from 1819 to 1827 and,
while his principles caused him to decline office in the
progressive Tory government of George Canning and Viscount
Goderich, his sense of duty led him unwillingly to become Prime
Minister in January 1828, but he presided over a divided
administration and lost support among its members. He alienated
many Tories by advising the House of Lords not to oppose the
repeal of the Test and Corporation Acts and lost the support of
the Canningites. In 1830 his declaration against parliamentary
reform brought about his fall from power. The mob hooted him on
the anniversary of Waterloo and broke the windows of his
residence, Apsley House.
     When William IV again called upon him to form a government, he
recommended Peel as Prime Minister and temporarily managed the
government during the three weeks until Peel was brought back
from Rome. He was Foreign Secretary in Peel's short-lived
administration; but when Peel returned to power in 1841 he held
no office except that of Commander-in-Chief. He supported Peel's
Corn Law legislation and, when the government was defeated in
1846, retired from public life.

385. Lord Stanhope, <u>Notes of Conversations with the Duke of
     Wellington, 1832-1852</u> (1889)

386. Sir Herbert Maxwell, <u>Life of Wellington</u> (2 vols., Sampson
     Low, 1900)

387. Hon. Sir John Fortescue, <u>Wellington</u> (Williams & Norgate, 1925)

388. C.R.M.F. Cruttwell, <u>Wellington</u> (Duckworth), 1936)

389. Seventh Duke of Wellington (ed)., <u>Wellington and his Friends</u> (Batsford, 1965)

390. Elizabeth Longford, <u>Wellington,Pillar of State</u> (Weidenfeld & Nicolson, 1972)

6

The Political Background

Eighteenth-century England was a brutal, callous society. This was shown in its delight in popular pastimes involving much inhumanity, cruelty and degradation, such as cock-fighting, bear-baiting, bull-running and prize-fighting. It was shown also in the savage and relentless nature of the penal law, which sought to deter offenders by reliance upon humiliating and public punishments inflicted by means of the whipping-post, ducking-stool, stocks and pillory. And recourse to such severity led to ever-harsher penalties. Thousands of convicted criminals were transported to servitude, first in the American colonies and then in Australia. Above all, increasing reliance was placed upon death by hanging (see no. 769). During the course of the century, Parliament raised the number of capital crimes from about fifty to nearly two hundred. These included picking a pocket to the value of a shilling (4p), stealing five shillings (25p) in a shop or on a navigable river, stealing forty shillings (£2) from a dwelling-house, cutting down a tree, stealing a sheep, stealing cloth from a bleaching-ground, sending a threatening letter, undermining the banks of a river, consorting with gypsies or setting fire to a haystack.

In practice, however, the death penalty was less and less carried out. Juries often refused to convict for petty offences, and when the death penalty was imposed, it was frequently commuted to transportation. By the early years of the nineteenth century, only one in twenty was executed of those condemned to death, and for shoplifting the proportion was one in 1,200. Capital punishment had become haphazard and largely ineffective. And by the early nineteenth century, a group of Whig humanitarians were seeking the reform of the law. At first they met with little success. Their first leader, Sir Samuel Romilly, succeeded only in persuading Parliament in 1808 to abolish the death penalty for picking pockets and stealing from bleaching grounds; but his successor, Sir James Mackintosh, secured the appointment of a parliamentary committee in 1819, which recommended the abolition of a considerable number of capital offences.

When Peel became Home Secretary in 1822, he made it clear that he agreed with most of the committee's proposals. Between 1822 and 1827 he was able to carry five statutes exempting over a hundred crimes from the death penalty and reducing the severity of the punishment for many others. He did not go as far as the Whig reformers would have liked; and he did not always accede to George IV's wish to commute capital sentences passed by the courts (see no. 648). His approach was more cautious because he wished first to see the effect of these and other reforms.

One of these concerned the prisons. These had not originally been intended as places of punishment for convicted offenders. Rather they were for the detention of persons awaiting trial, who would be liable to capital and other penalties. The Poor Law of 1601 empowered Justices of the Peace to establish houses of correction (commonly known as Bridewells from the name of the former royal residence in which the first one was establishedin London) in which 'sturdy beggars' could be detained and 'inured to labour.' During the eighteenth century it became the practice for Justices to sentence minor offenders and debtors both to these places and to prisons, and the two sorts of institutions became largely the same.

The prisons throughout the country, though mainly the responsibility of the Justices, were inadequately controlled and financed. Jailers often had unrestricted powers over their prisoners, who might have to pay them to be free of shackles and receive better food and accommodation. Many buildings were dilapidated, crowded and unhealthy. Men and women, young and old, convicted and untried, all often lived and slept together with little supervision. From the later eighteenth century a number of reformers, notably John Howard (1726-1790) and Elizabeth Fry (1780-1845), investigated them and made the abuses known.

Peel had been deeply influenced by their revelations, and he wished to initiate reforms because prison sentences would now have to be imposed for offences formerly punished by the death penalty. In 1823 and 1824 his measures provided that each county and large town was to have its own prison, administered by the Justices of the Peace, who were also to inspect them regularly; that their upkeep, including the wages of the jailers, were to be paid out of local rates; that women prisoners were to have women jailers; that chaplains and surgeons were to be appointed to the prisons; and that prisoners were to be graded for work and receive religious instruction and elementary education. He opposed the abolition of the punishment of whipping because he believed that it and the revised prison system made 'an effective secondary punishment.'

While Peel was inclined to be cautious in his judicial and prison reforms, he was more advanced than the opinion of most people in his determination to secure the better enforcement of the law, which still rested fundamentally upon the provisions of the Statute of Winchester of 1285, and this in itself largely reaffirmed the practice of past centuries. Every freeman was liable to serve for a year in his parish or township as an unpaid constable responsible for maintaining the peace of the locality and taking wrongdoers to be tried by the Justices. It became common, however,for communities to hire watchmen to perform these duties. They were commonly aged paupers, unwilling and unable to act effectively.

As towns grew in size, their means of preserving law and order became so impotent that crime flourished almost unchecked and rioting became endemic. The situation was particularly serious in London. In about 1750 the novelist Henry Fielding, London first paid magistrate,established at the Bow Street Court a group of 'thief-takers,' who became known as the Bow Street

Runners, but their function was to detect crime, not to prevent
it. Crime steadily increased in the capital, and in 1828 it was
estimated that one Londoner in every 383 was a criminal.

After the brief interval (between April 1827 and January
1828) during his period as Home Secretary, Peel secured the
passing of the Metropolitan Police Act of 1829. This set up a
paid police force for the built-up area of London (ecluding the
old City) under two Commissioners with its headquarters at
Scotland Yard (see no. 650) and an initial strength of 3,000 men.
There was considerable public opposition to the introduction of
a police force, which was associated with foreign patterns of
military despotism. To emphasize its civilian character its
members were armed only with truncheons and wore blue tailcoats
and tophats.

The benefits of the new force were soon apparent. There was an
immediate marked and steady decline in crime throughout the
metropolitan area. Within a few years all hostility to this
reform ceased. The contrast with the situation in the provinces
made further action necessary, especially as criminals now moved
from London to the unpoliced areas. The Municipal Corporations
Act of 1835 made possible the establishment of police forces in
the boroughs and the County Police Act of 1839 in the counties.
By the time of Peel's death, most parts of the country had police
forces based upon the example of the Metropolitan Force.

391. Sidney & Beatrice Webb, English Prisons (Longmans, 1922)

392. C. Dilnot, Scotland Yard: Its History and Organization
(new edition, Geoffrey Bles, 1929)

393. C. Reith, A Short History of the British Police (OUP,
1948)

394. L. Radzinowicz, History of English Criminal Law (Stevens
& Son, 1948)

395. J.M. Hart, The British Police (Macmillan,1951)

396. V.A.C. Batrell, The Hanging Tree, Execution and the
English People, 1770-1868 (OUP, 1994)

POLITICS AND REFORM

By the later part of the seventeenth century the development of a
parliamentary monarchy in England had produced a party system.
The two parties that emerged each became known by the hostile
nickname it had acquired - 'Tory' being a term originally used to
describe Irish brigands and 'Whig' to describe Scottish
Covenanters (or Presbyterian rebels). They were political
groups contesting with each other for power and disagreeing over
the political and religious issues of the day. Traditionally the
Tories championed the cause of the Established Church, the Crown
and the landed gentry, while the Whigs were for the Dissenters,
Parliament and the commercial classes.

These party differences tended to become largely quiescent
during the eighteenth century, but by the begining of the next
century they were reviving, being stimulated by the consequences
of two dissimilar revolutions - the ideological effects of the
French Revolution and the social effects of the Industrial

Revolution - and crystallizing into the great political issue of parliamentary reform, which meant making the House of Commons more representative of the nation.

The House of Commons, as inherited from the past, was unrepresentative in three ways. First, the distribution of both county and borough seats, each of which returned two members to Parliament, was haphazard and out-of-date. The southern counties were vastly over-represented in proportion to their populatiion and wealth; the boroughs included many small and declining villages, while important new and growing industrial towns, such as Birmingham, Leeds and Manchester, were unrepresented. Second, the right to vote was arbitrary. In the counties it was confined to men possessing freehold property valued at forty shillings (£2) a year; in the boroughs there was no uniformity, but in most of them the electors were only a small proportion of the inhabitants. Third, in many boroughs and some counties a few wealthy or otherwise powerful men could control elections by influence or corruption. Seats were openly recognized as property; and Peel's political career was founded upon this practice.

The Whigs, as representing the tradition of parliamentary government and the aspirations of the Dissenters and new industrial classes, became the party of reform. When Lord Grey, who belonged to an aristocratic Whig family, came into power in 1830, the aim of the party was to effect such a measure of reform as would enfranchise those classes likely to support them in the future. The main proposals of their Reform Bill of 1832 were to disfranchise many of the small boroughs, to give members to the most important of the large towns and more members to some populous counties and to establish a uniform franchise (to be possessed by householders occupying a building worth at least £10 a year) in all boroughs and slightly extend the suffrage in the counties.

The introduction of the Reform Bill presented Peel with a crisis. What was to be his attitude towards it? He opposed it, but not as thoroughly as did Wellington and the 'Ultra Tories' (see no. 837). He upheld the existing constitution, though accepting that it needed some reform; but he considered that the Bill was extreme and dangerously likely to encourage demands for further change and upset the country's system of government (no. 836)

He fully recognized, however, that the House of Commons possessed a majority of members in favour of reform and rioting in several towns indicated popular support for it. He would not, therefore, contemplate supporting attempts to restrict the measures of the Bill as a compromise measure. When, therefore, during the famous 'Days of May' in 1832, after Grey had resigned following the King's refusal to create sufficient new peers to secure the passing of the Bill in the House of Lords, he refused to join a Tory government which would pass a reduced Reform Bill (no. 845). This made it impossible for Wellington to form such an administration, and the King had to accept the Whigs back on their own terms. The Bill was passed, and Peel indicated the terms on which he accepted it.

It was during the early 1830's that the new term 'Conservative' began to replace 'Tory' as the appellation of the party (no. 847). Peel welcomed this as meaning in essence that a fresh party had emerged as a result of the attitude he had taken during the controversy over parliamentary reform. He regarded it as a wider party seeking to save what was valuable from the past and ensure that any necessary change developed peacefully from the past rather than destroying it violently. . It was about this time too that the term 'Liberal' was applied the Radicals among the Whigs and was later extended to the whole party.

397. J.R.M. Butler, The Passing of the Great Reform Bill
     (Longmans, 1914)

398. Charles Seymour, Electoral Reform in England and Wales,
     1832 - 1885 (Department of History, Yale Historical
     Productions, Yale University, 1915; reprinted with an
     introduction by M. Hurst, 1970)

399. R.L. Hill, Toryism and the People, 1832-1846 (Constable,
     1929)

400. N. Gash,'English Reform and the French Revolution in
     the General Election of 1830,' R.Pares & A.J.P.Taylor
     (eds.), Essays Presented to Sir Lewis Namiier
          (Macmillan, 1956),pp. 258-288

401. Geoffrey B.A.M. Finlayson, England in the Eighteen
     Thirties, Decade of Reform (Edward Arnold, 1969)

402. Alan Beatie (ed.), English Party Politics (2 vols.,
     Weidenfeld & Nicolson, 1970), Vol. I, 1600-1906.

403. Derek Beales, The Parliamentary Parties of Nineteenth-
     Century Britain (Historical Association, 1971)

404. Robert Stewart, The Foundation of the Conservative
     Party,1830-1867 Longmans, 1978)

405. Frank O'Gorman, The Emergence of the British Two-Party
     System (Edward Arnold, 1982)

406. Robert Blake, The Conservative Party from Peel to
     Thatcher (Fontana, 1985)

407. Eric J. Evans, Political Parties in Britain, 1783-1867
     (Lancaster Pamphlets, Methuen, 1985)

408. B.W. Hill, British Parliamentary Parties, 1742-1832
     (Allen & Unwin, 1985)

THE CHURCH OF ENGLAND

During the eighteenth century, the religious position in England rested upon the generally-accepted 'settlement in Church and State,' which had followed the Glorious Revolution of 1688. This maintained and even strengthened the dominant position of the Church of England in the constitution. It remained the Established Church of the land. Its bishops continued to sit in the House of Lords as spiritual peers. The Bill of Rights required the monarch to be a member of it.The two universities and the endowed schools were under its control.
     The Act of Toleration of 1689 had granted freedom of worship to Protestant Dissenters, but the Corporation Act of 1661 and the

Test Act of 1673 still required all members of Parliament and of municipal corporations and holders of office under the Crown to communicate annually according to the rites of the Church, but, in fact, infringement of these two acts had been covered since 1727 by the passing of an annual Act of Indemnity. Roman Catholics were also affected by this legislation and could not obtain relief through the Act of Indemnity; and they had not obtained legal freedom of worship, though in practice this was generally tolerated.

By the beginning of the nineteenth century, the growth of Methodism had greatly added to the numbers of Dissenters, and the part they now took in trade and industry steadily increased their importance in the life of the country. While recognizing that the Test and Corporation Acts had become virtually symbolic, Dissenters had come to resent the social inferiority implied by their existence. Public and parliamentary opinion increasingly supported them, and in 1828 Wellington's government repealed these acts. Peel, though considering it inexpedient, had to accept the measure, and as Home Secretary virtually took charge of its successful passage into law (see no. 804).

The repeal of the Test and Corporation Acts would probably have come earlier if it had not been for the Roman Catholic question. There was no logical reason why Roman Catholics should not be given the same degree of toleration as Protestant Dissenters, but this had not got the support of British public opinion, which still held its traditional suspicion of them. Moreover, the position was complicated by the position of Ireland with its predominately Roman Catholic population.

Nevertheless, it was Ireland that precipitated the adoption of Roman Catholic Emancipation. In 1823 O'Connell had founded the Catholic Association to secure emancipation;   it was becoming more powerful, and at a by-election in 1828 he was returned to Parliament for County Clare. Since the law prevented him taking his seat, this presented Wellington's government with a challenge. Wellington believed that only emancipation could prevent a civil war. Peel was placed in a particularly difficult position. The University of Oxford was a stronghold of both the Church of England and the Tory party, and a speech he had made in the House of Commons in 1817, in which he had opposed concessions being made to Roman Catholics, had contributed towards his election as a Member of Parliament for the University. He decided, however, that he must support his Prime Minister, and again as Home Secretary secured the passage of the requisite measure through Parliament (see no. 804).

He resigned his University seat and was defeated when he stood again for re-election, but was able to remain in Parliament by securing another rotten borough. Peel was widely regarded as having betrayed the Protestant cause, but in the general election of 1834 he set out to prove that he was a sincere member of the Church of England by stating in the Tamworth Manifesto that he would reform its weaknesses and abuses, which were crippling its mission and laying it open to attack by its opponents.

These were age-long in their origin and still existed largely because the English Reformation had not been as thoroughgoing as that on the Continent or in Scotland. The temporal authority of the Papacy over the Church of England was then transferred to the Crown, the monasteries were dissolved, the clergy were allowed to marry, the services were anglicized and changed and a

moderate doctrinal position was adopted in relation to the
theological controversies of the sixteenth century. Otherwise
the government and organization of the Church and its connection
with the State remained substantially as it had been during the
Middle Ages including the accompanying abuses.

Among the most serious of these was the use made of
ecclesiastical patronage. Medieval monarchs had vied with popes
to possess control of appointments in the Church, especially of
the higher clergy, in order to requite the services of their
ministers (who were clerics) with ecclesiastical posts; and the
elimination of papal power at the Reformation settlement
increased their unchallenged patronage. In the later
seventeenth century after the Civil War, this power was
transferred from the Crown to Parliament and used to secure and
reward clerical support for political purposes. In particular,
the votes of the bishops in the House of Lords were valuable to a
government; and during the greater part of the eighteenth
century, when Whig administrations predominated, only Whig
clergymen could expect to be made bishops.

The first politician to make a proper, non-political use of
ecclesiastical patronage was Lord Liverpool when he was Prime
Minister from 1812 to 1827. During that time he took the
initiative in considering only the suitability of clergymen for
the appointments he made, regardless of any political advantage
that might be gained from them. In this he was scrupulously
followed by Peel, who also introduced important reforms in the
life and organization of the Church.

One of these was in the realm of finance. Lord Henley, Peel's
brother-in-law, wrote a very influential pamphlet, A Plan of
Church Reform, in 1832. In this he praised Lord Liverpool because
'disregarding the powerful, he elevated unpretending merit and
excellence to high places in the Church.' Furthermore, he gave
his attention to the condition of the Church's income, which was
seriously chaotic and inadequate, a situation also inherited
from the Middle Ages. He advocated the establishment of a body to
manange efficiently the estates and revenues of the Church, and
this was among the reforms subsequently undertaken by Peel.

In 1835 Peel established an Ecclesiastical Duties and Revenue
Commission, which produced its report in the following year,
when it was reconstituted as the Ecclesiastical Commission, a
permanent body consisting of bishops, officers of state and
laymen, that was charged with the reform and management of the
Church's financial structure. Among the reforms it undertook
were equalising bishops' revenues (1836), restrictions on
pluralism (1838) and suppressing the excess revenues of
cathedrals for redistribution among parishes (1840).

Another serious weakness of the Church was its slowness in
providing for the growing populations of the expanding
industrial towns. A vital reason for this was that, while the
dissenting bodies could build new places of worship without any
restriction, the Church always had to go through the lengthy and
costly process of securing the passage of an Act of Parliament
for the creation of a new parish. In 1843 the Populous Parishes
Act allowed the formation of separate districts (commonly known
as 'Peel parishes') out of existing parishes even where a church
did not already exist. In the past Parliament had granted
moneytowards the building of new churches, but Peel realized
that dissenting opinion would no longer countenance this. He
gave £4,000 towards church building in London and the

industrial areas (The Times, 11th. October 1843); and the
Ecclesiastical Commission was empowered to borrow up to £600,000
towards the stipends of the clergy in these new districts.

The most active member of the Ecclesiastical Commission was
Charles James Blomfield, Bishop of London from 1828 to 1856, who
co-operated closely with Peel's ecclesiastical measures. In
particular, some 200 new churches were built in his diocese
during his episcopate,and his efforts were emulated by other
bishops. It has been said that the Church of England was saved in
the nineteenth century by three men - Liverpool, Peel and
Blomfield.

409. Memoirs of the Public Life and Administration of the Rt.
     Hon. the Earl of Liverpool (1827)

410. G.E. Biber, Bishop Blomfield and his Times (Harrison,
     1857)

411. S.C. Carpenter, Church and People, 1789-1889
     (SPCK, 1933)

412. J.W.C. Wand, The Second Reform (Faith Press, 1953)

413. Olive J. Brose, Church and Parliament: The Reshaping of
     the Church of England, 1828-1860 (Stanford University
     Press, 1959)

414. G.F.A. Best, 'The Whigs and the Church Establishment in
     the Age of Grey and Holland,' History, vol. LI. (June
     1960), pp. 133-148

415. P.J. Welch, 'Blomfield and Peel: A Study in Co-operation
     between Church and State, 1841 - 1846,' Journal of
     Ecclesiastical History vol. XII (1961), pp. 71-84

416. G.F.A. Best, Temporal Pillars: Queen Anne's Bounty, the
     Ecclesiastical Commissioners and the Church of England
     (SPCK, 1964)

417. O. Chadwick, The Victorian Church (Black,1966),

418. E.R. Norman, Church and Society in England, 1770-1970
     (OUP, 1976)

THE BANK OF ENGLAND

The Bank of England was founded in 1694 primarily in order to
enable the government to finance the wars against Louis XIV's
France. A number of merchants and financiers in London lent the
government £1,200,000 for which it paid £100,000 a year. This was
a low rate of interest, but in return the lenders received a
charter incorporating them as the Governor and Company of the
Bank of England. Among its privileges was the right of being the
only joint-stock bank empowered to issue notes in and around
London. These notes soon became an essential part of the national
currency, and in order to secure financial stability, it was
required that the total value of the notes issued must represent
the amount of gold held by the Bank.

In 1797,however, the Younger Pitt's government, facing a

financial crisis in the war against revolutionary France, relieved the Bank from this obligation. This was intended to be a temporary measure, but it was continued for the duration of the war. The result was the virtual disappearance of gold from circulation and the appearance of a paper currency which steadily fell in value. In 1810 the House of Commons appointed a Committee of Inquiry into the situation. It produced the next year a Bullion Report, which recommended a resumption of the gold standard, but Nicholas Vansittart, who was then the Chancellor of the Exchequer, secured its rejection by a large majority.

When hostilities ended in 1815, the situation remained unchanged bringing about continuing inflation, which contributed towards the post-war depression and resulted in especial hardship for the poor as prices inevitably rose faster than wages. This time both Houses of Parliament appointed Committees of Inquiry. Peel was chosen to be the chairman of the House of Commons Committee. He had voted against the adoption of the Report of 1811, but this time (having now read it for the first time), he changed his outlook and decided that its recommemdations should be carried out. He persuaded the Committee to support him, and in 1819 Parliament passed 'Peel's Act' (as it was called), which secured the return of the British currency to the gold standard.

The Act,however, suffered from serious limitations. It had restored the gold standard, but this time it had not ensured that there should be sufficient gold to cover the notes issued. There was no legal restriction upon the issue of paper money by the Bank,and the situation was made worse by the existence now of over four hundred private banks, each of which was allowed to issue its own notes. Peel set out to remedy this by the Bank Charter Act of 1844, which gave the Bank the responsibilities of a 'central bank' managing the currency for the government. It was also to be a 'lender of last resort' to assist private bankers, financiers and merchants in difficulties. The Act acted against inflation by limiting to a small sum the Bank's power to print notes apart from those backed by gold in the Bank's possession. It could issue notes without limit if backed by gold, but otherwise it could only issue £14,000,000 in notes against government securities. Other note-issuing banks were limited in number to those then in existence. If two such banks amalgamated with each other, they both lost their right to issue notes; and two-thirds of their lost issue was to be added to that of the Bank of England, while the rest was to lapse.

The ultimate purpose of the Act was to make the Bank of England the only bank of issue in England and Wales, and this object was finally attained in 1921, when the last of the note-issuing private banks was absorbed by one of the greater banks. The restrictions it imposed upon the issue of bank-notes made them relatively unimportant in financial transactions, and the use of cheques spread. Above all, the stringent form of gold standard it upheld was to be the basis of the British monetary system until 1914.

419. H.T. Easton, History and Principles of Banks and Banking (Effingham Wilson, 1924)

420. Sir J.H. Clapham, The Bank of England (CUP, 2 vols., 1938)

421. Sir T.E. Gregory, <u>Select Statutes, Documents and Reports</u>
     <u>Relating to British Banking, 1832-1928</u> (OUP, 1929)

422. R.S. Sayers, <u>Central Banking after Bagehot</u> (OUP, 1957)

423. Sir R.G. Hawtrey, <u>The Centenary of the Bank Rate</u>
     (Frank Cass, 1962)

424. A. Feaveryear, <u>The Pound Sterling, A History of</u>
     <u>English Money</u> (OUP, 1963)

425. G.G. Riley, 'Peel and the Bank Act, 1844,' <u>Institute</u>
     <u>Bankers Journal</u> (February 1963)

IMPERIAL AND FOREIGN POLICY

Peel's importance in British domestic affairs has meant that most historians have tended to neglect his overseas policies. And, indeed, during his earlier political career under Wellington and as leader of the opposition, he had shown little interest in overseas matters, and when he became Prime Minister in 1841, Wellington thought that he knew nothing about such matters, though the French politician, François Guizot (1787-1874), spoke more favourably of him (no. 1152)

Nevertheless, when he came into power that year, Britain as the victor in the Napoleonic Wars, the leading industrial nation in the world and the possessor of the largest navy, was a European state that was bound to exercise an important influence in the affairs of the Continent. Moreover, the British Empire was now expanding across the world and bringing for the government a succession of opportunities and problems. Peel, therefore, could not ignore overseas questions and was involved in a number of issues which required his consideration. And he showed, whatever may have been his attitude in the past, that he was able to understand them and adopt a definite policy towards them which gained him considerable success.

426. <u>Cambridge History of British Foreign Policy</u>, vol. II,
     (CUP, 1923)

427. W.P. Morrell, <u>British Colonial Policy in the Age of</u>
     <u>Peel and Russell</u> (OUP, 1930)

Europe

In Europe always the most important question still to be faced for the greater part of the nineteenth century was the age-long relationship of Britain with her nearest Continental neighbour across the Channel - France. The rise of France in the seventeenth century to the position of a great power, able to dominate the Continent and set out to gain an overseas empire, had been challenged by Britain and resulted in a series of extensive wars fought between the two countries during the eighteenth century.

These had culminated in victory for Britain in 1815, a victory that meant, in fact, that the French claim to supremacy in Europe was over. This, however, was not immediately apparent. Not until the defeat of France in the Franco-Prussian War of 1870 and the establishment of German unity by Bismarck was France's dominance undoubtedly overthrown. For the entire period of Peel's premiership France remained the country that could supremely affect the fortunes of her neighbours. As Guizot truly remarked, 'When France has a cold, Europe sneezes!'

When Peel became Prime Minister in 1841, France had undergone, over a decade before, a second revolution, which this time was peaceful in contrast to the violent revolution set off by the storming of the Bastille in 1789. When Britain and her allies had overthrown Napoleon they had sought to put the clock back and restored the old monarchy in the person of King Louis XVIII, a younger brother of the executed Louis XVI. He set out to restore the absolutism of of the old régime, a policy which was continued by Charles X, who succeeded him in 1824. This eventually led to his forced abdication in 1830 and his replacement by King Louis-Philippe of the Orleanist line of the monarchy. Peel agreed with his Foreign Secretary, Lord Aberdeen, in wishing for peaceful relations with France. In 1842 he and Guizot proclaimed an Entente Cordiale , which was intended to be a friendly agreement between the two countries, though not an alliance.

Peel showed himself, however, more determined than Aberdeen to resist any attempts at French aggression. Louis-Philippe was anxious to strengthen his position on the throne by re-asserting his country's position in Europe, a policy which he knew French public opinion would welcome. He saw an opportunity of doing this offered to him by the situation in Spain. The marriages of Queen Isabella of Spain and her younger sister had for some time been a matter of international discussion. The idea of the Queen marrying a French prince aroused in Britain the same fear of a union between the French and Spanish crowns that had brought about the War of the Spanish Succession (1701-1713). Eventually the British and French governments agreed that she should marry her cousin Francis; but in 1844 it was rumoured that Louis-Philippe intended to marry his youngest son, the Duke of Monpensier, to the Queen's sister. Since the Queen was not expected to have children, this was intended to bring an Orleanist heir to the Spanish throne. Aberdeen was prepared to accept this, but Peel strongly condemned it (see no.1024). Louis-Philippe then arranged that, simultaneously with the Queen's wedding, his son should marry her sister. This was an empty victory, since the Queen soon had a son, and it resulted in the deterioration of Anglo-French relations which Peel had feared.

Another disagreement between Peel and Aberdeen was over the question of national defence. Though the country's armed forces had been steadily run down since 1815, Aberdeen did not want to provoke France by bringing them up to a more effective standard. Peel, however, thought that French policy decreed otherwise, especially with regard to Britain's all-important naval strength. In addition, this was the age when iron and steam were replacing wood and sail in the construction of warships. The French had become pioneers in this; they did not have the conservative pride of the British in the victories won by their old men-o-war. Peel listened to the urgent pleas of the reformers in the navy, and in 1845 his government embarked upon the expenditure of a million pounds on the navy, which included the construction of a number of 'iron frigates.' This made possible the maintenance of the naval supremacy upon which British foreign policy relied throughout the century.

428. J.Hall, <u>England and the Orleans Monarchy</u> (Longmans, 1912)

429. R.Guyot, <u>La Première Entente Cordiale</u> (Paris, 1926)

430. E. Jones Parry, <u>The Spanish Marriages,1841-1846</u> (Macmillan, 1936)

431. R.W. Seton Watson, <u>Britain in Europe, 1789-1914: A Survey of Foreign Policy</u> (CUP, 1937)

432. M.S. Anderson, <u>The Ascendancy of Europe, Aspects of European History, 1815-1914</u> (Macmillan,1972)

India

The story of the British in India began in 1600 when Queen Elizabeth I issued a charter establishing the East India Company and granting it a monopoly of trade in the East. The Company wished primarily to trade with the islands of Sumatra and Java, from which valuable spices were to be obtained, but in 1624 the rival Dutch East India Company compelled it to withdraw from this area, and it diverted its efforts to the Indian mainland. By 1690 it had established 'factories' (trading-stations) at Madras, Bombay and Calcutta. During the next century, the need to protect its interests, to establish its suzerainty over native princes following the collapse of the Mogul Empire and to defeat French ambitions in India led it to acquiring and governing large territories in the peninsula. Consequently it departed increasingly from its position as a commercial country and had to concentrate upon collecting taxes and maintaining soldiers.

The development of this situation raised the problem of the relationship between the British government and the Company in the administration of its Indian territories. Pitt by his India Act of 1784 sought to settle this by a division of responsibility between the two. This set up a Board of Control for Indian affairs under a President in London, but in 1816 this ceased to meet, and its power was exercised by its President alone. Government in India was in the hands of a Governor-General appointed by the Cabinet. The Court of Directors of the Company (set up by the original charter) retained control of its commercial activities and Indian patronage, but its trading activities declined, and in 1833 it relinquished all these and confined itself to civil and military administration and patronage.

In administering India, successive British governments were placed in a very difficult position. The Governor-General was virtually in control of the sub-continent, and since communication between him and the government in London took three months to travel the ten thousand miles each way, the government could in practice do little but accept his decisions and concur with his actions. Lord Auckland was Governor-General at the beginning of Peel's premiership. He had embarked upon the conquest of Afghanistan with the avowed purpose of checking Russian intervention there. His term of office expired in 1842, and Peel replaced him by Lord Ellenborough. He arrived in India to hear that the Afghans had risen, captured Kabul, the capital, massacred the British garrison with the exception of a single survivor and taken the women and children prisoners. Ellenborough ordered the evacuation of the country without any attempt to rescue the prisoners; but the officers commanding the frontier ignored the order. They recaptured Kabul, rescued the prisoners and accomplished a successful retreat.

When the affair became known in England, the Whigs vehemently criticized Ellenborough in Parliament, but Peel defended him. Then came Ellenborough's action in the province of Sind, through which the British force had passed to invade Afghanistan. He decided that its rulers were not sufficiently well-disposed towards Britain and resolved to annex it. Sir Charles Napier, who was employed in the army of the East India Company, willingly undertook this and triumphantly telegraphed his success in Latin - 'Pecavi' ('I have sinned'), but Ellenborough was considered in England to have acted unjustly and harshly. The Court of Directors of the Company, alarmed by his bellicosity, demanded his recall in 1843. Peel continued to support him, but the next year he went on to annex Gwalior, where disorder was prevalent, and Peel had to agree that he should relinquish his office.

As his successor, Peel secured the appointment of a military figure, Sir Henry Hardinge, who was a veteran of the Peninsular campaign against Napoleon, but was ready to follow a pacific policy in India. Nevertheless, he found that the Punjab, under the rule of the Sikhs, was even more disturbed than Gwalior and threatening to attack British India. He did not act until the threat actually materialized. The he defeated the Sikh army in a hard-fought battle. This event might well have justified the annexation of the Punjab, but Hardinge respected Peel's moderate policy. He merely established a friendly government there and then withdrew the British troops.

Peel's wish for moderation and peace in India was probably not as realistic in the circumstances as Ellenborough's policy of firmness and territorial expansion. The Punjab, for instance, was again in turmoil within less than three years and had to be annexed by Hardinge's successor. Yet Peel's views were in accordance with the contemporary British outlook. No one in Britain cared about triumphs in Sind or Afghanistan, he told Hardinge and recommended him to follow peaceful constructive policies instead (M.E. Yapp, Strategies of British India, p. 521). By 1854 the outbreak of the Crimean War was to reveal an aggressive, bellicose development in British public opinion, but he could hardly be blamed for not foreseeing this.

433. P. Auber, An Analysis of the Constitution of the East India Company (1826)

434. Sir John Kaye, History of the War in Afghanistan (1851)

435. Sir Alfred Lyall, The Rise and Expansion of the British Dominion in India (John Murray, 5th. edn., 1910)

436. P.E. Roberts, A History of British India under the Company and the Crown (OUP, 1923)

537. Vincent A. Smith, The Oxford History of India (OUP, 2nd. edn., 1941)

538. Patrick Macrory, Signal Catastrophe, The Story of the Disastrous Retreat from Kabul, 1842 (Hodder & Stoughton, 1966)

539. M.E. Yapp, <u>Strategies of British India, 1798-1850</u>
(OUP, 1980)

North America

By 1841 several disputes between Britain and the United States
had strained relations between the two countries. The oldest of
these concerned the boundary between Maine and New Brunswick.
This had been submitted in 1831 to the arbitration of the King of
the Netherlands, but the American Senate rejected his decision.
Even more serious was the Oregon question. In 1818 the Canadian-
American frontier had been fixed along the parallel of 49 degrees
North, but not as far as what was then termed Oregon, which
comprised as well the present state those also of Idaho and
Washington and the Canadian province of British Columbia. Both
Britain and America had long claimed the whole of this territory,
and in 1818 a temporary joint occupation had been agreed upon,
but the activities of both the Hudson's Bay Company and American
pioneers made this increasingly unstable.

The effect of these boundary disputes was made worse by two
other questions. The British government, having abolished
slavery throughout the Empire in 1833, maintained a naval
squadron off the coast of West Africa to prevent the slave trade,
and several European governments recognized its right to search
suspected ships at sea. Though the United States was not a party
to this agreement, British warships insisted upon inspecting
ships flying the American flag to ensure that they were not
slavers sailing under false colours. American opinion resented
this, and early in 1841 Congress accepted a report by the
Committee on Foreign Affairs calling for greater efforts to
protect American ships.

To this was added an incident during the Canadian rebellion of
1837 when an American steamer, the <u>Caroline</u>, conveying arms to
the rebels was captured and destroyed by loyalists on the St.
Lawrence River; and in the spring of 1841 a British subject,
M'Leod, was arrested in New York and charged with having killed
an American on the ship during the episode. When tried for
murder, he was acquitted, but feeling in Canada and Britain ran
very high.

Peel's reaction in opposition to the M'Leod affair was
bellicose (see no.1022); and in October 1841 he issued as Prime
Minister a cabinet memorandum stating that'some immediate and
decisive demonstration on our part may be necessary.' The naval
strength at Gibraltar and Halifax, Nova Scotia, was increased,
and preparations were made to send reinforcements to Bermuda if
necessary.

Peel wished, however, to settle the boundary disputes. As
with India, he saw no advantage in Britain gaining more
territory there, especially by enlarging the empty lands of
Canada. In 1842 Lord Ashburton was sent to Washington to settle
with Daniel Webster, the Secretary of State, the Maine dispute.
The result was the Webster-Ashburton Treaty, which awarded the
United States much the same territory as the King of the
Netherlands had formerly proposed. At the same time, in return
for the American government sending a naval squadron to the
African coast, Britain recognized the protection of 'regularly
documented ships' by the flag they flew.

By now the Oregon question had become more serious as growing
numbers of American settlers entered the territory

and began to demand the seizure of the entire area up to 54.40
degrees, the southern boundary of Alaska. When James Polk became
President in 1845 he supported this demand, and there arose the
cry of '54.40 or Fight!' Peel had already decided upon a
determined stand against the American demand (see no. 1022). He
knew that Polk, indeed, who was on the verge of war against
Mexico, did not want war; and the President accepted the British
proposal that the boundary should be 49 degrees North with a
deviation to allow Vancouver Island to go to Cananda. The
settlement was proclaimed on the same day as Peel announced the
resignation of his government in 1846.

540. B. De Voto, <u>Year of Decision,1846</u> (Macmillan Co.,
    New York, 1943)

541. R.E. Riegel, <u>America Moves West</u> (Henry Holt & Co., New
    York, revised edition, 1947)

542. F. Merk, <u>Albert Gallatin and the Oregon Problem</u> (Harvard
    University Press, Cambridge, 1950)

THE CORN LAWS

During the mid sixteenth and later seventeenth centuries,
economic policy in western European countries was largely
governed by a system which was later called 'mercantilism' by
Adam Smith. This believed in intervention by governments in
order to encourage exports and limit imports and so increase both
the wealth and power of their states. The most common way of doing
this was by imposing duties upon imported goods; and duties were
also imposed upon native products as a convenient way of raising
money for a government. This policy was more and more put into
effect in Britain until by the later eighteenth century there
were few articles that were not taxed in this way.
    Sydney Smith (1771-1845) memorably declared that there were
'taxes upon every article which enters the mouth or covers the
back or is placed under the foot; taxes upon everything which it
is pleasant to see, hear, feel, smell or taste; taxes upon
warmth, light and locomotion; taxes on the raw material; taxes on
every fresh value that is added to it by the industry of man;
taxes on the sauce which pampers appetite and the drug that
restores health; on the ermine which decorates the judge and the
rope which hangs the criminal; on the poor man's salt and the rich
man's spice; on the brass nails of the coffin and the ribbons of
the bride - at bed or board, downlying or uprising, we must pay.
The schoolboy whips his taxed top; the beardless youth manages
his taxed horse with a taxed bridle on a taxed road;   and the
dying Englishman, pouring his medicine, which has paid 7 per
cent, into a spoon that has paid 15 per cent, flings himself back
upon his chintz bed, which has paid 22 per cent, and expires in
the arms of an apothcary who has paid a license of £100 for the
privilege of putting him to death...' - Quoted , M.B. Synge,
<u>A Short History of Social Life in England</u> (Hodder & Stoughton,
1906), pp. 363-364; L.C.B. Seaman, <u>Victorian England</u>
(Routledge, 1973), p. 79.
    It was Adam Smith (1723-179) who first effectively criticized
the economic system to which he gave a name. In his book, <u>The
Wealth of Nations</u>, published in 1776, he severely condemned

mercantilism as a short-sighted, mistaken policy. He argued that the exchange of goods was governed by mutual needs and brought mutual benefits and that, therefore, artificial restrictions on free and natural course of trade were harmful to the interests of all participating nations. If trade were left free, nations would supply each other's requirements, so that 'the different states into which a great continent was divided would so resemble the different provinces of a great empire.'

The American War of Independence weakened faith in Britain in the mercantilist system, and the worldwide productive supremacy gained by British industry began to change the situation uniqely for it. As Adam Smith observed, 'our merchants and manufacturers have been by far the principal architects of the (mercantilist) system,' but now the changed situation made them advocates of free trade. They now needed to be able to obtain their raw materials as cheaply as possible and to dispose of their much-needed goods without impediment and feared no foreign competition. Even if the removal of British restrictions did not encourage other nations to do the same, vast and unprotected markets for their products lay elsewhere in the tropics and sub-tropics.

The Younger Pitt was influenced by The Wealth of Nations to take the first steps towards freer trade. In 1785 he reduced some customs duties, and the next year he made a commercial treaty with France which promised benefits to English factories and French vineyards. The Revolutionary and Napoleonic Wars checked this liberation of trade, and Parliament's refusal in 1816 to continue the wartime income tax prevented further reductions in general taxation; but commercial circles continued to ask for free trade and lower impositions on goods.

The first substantial abrogation of the mercantile system was achieved by William Huskisson, when he was at the Board of Trade from 1823 to 1827. His budget of 1824, the first in the century to lower tariffs, substituted moderate for prohibitive duties on raw wool and silk, and later he extended this to other imports. Since, however, later the Whig government elected in 1830 was more interested in constitutional than economic reform, further action against the control of trade was delayed.

The movement was cautiously renewed by Peel in his first budget of 1842. This brought about an all-round reduction of duties, including those on imported raw materials to 5%, on semi-manufactured goods to 12% and on manufactured goods to 20%. To replace the loss of revenue this caused the government, he introduced income tax at the rate of 7d. (3p.) in £1 on all incomes over £150 a year. He continued this policy in subsequent years and by 1846 had repealed the duties on 605 imported articles and lowered many others.

By then, however, this gradual process had been overtaken by a crisis in the operation of measures levying a particular import duty - the Corn Laws. During the Revolutionary and Napoleonic Wars, the French blockade of Britain and the poor harvest which occurred in those years had kept the price of corn high enough to preserve farming profits. The coming of peace, however, and an excellent harvest in 1815 brought about a quick and dramatic decline in the price of corn. The landed classes became alarmed. There had been a great increase in arable farming during the wars. Now farmers could not get an economic return for their grain, and landowners feared that their tenants would not be able to pay their rents.

Accordingly Parliament in 1815 passed an Act forbidding the importation of foreign corn into the United Kingdom until the domestic price reached 80 shillings (£2) a quarter. Corn prices, however, remained too low to bring farmers a reasonable profit, and Huskisson in 1828 responded to the agitation of the landed classes by replacing the existing scheme of prohibition by a sliding scale of duties depending upon the price of corn. This new system had no remarkable effect. Corn prices remained stable, largely because good harvests enabled arable farming to do well until 1836 when a series of bad harvests followed.

This stimulated agitation for the repeal of the Corn Laws. The Anti-Corn Law League came into existence in 1839 being founded in Manchester, the centre of the cotton industry. It was the manufacturers who wanted cheap food to assuage demands for higher wages by their workpeople, while the landed classes demanded protection for those whose profits depended upon their cereal production. The Whigs adopted the cause of the industrialists and free trade, and the Tories were the party of the landowners and protection.

Peel, therefore, was the leader of the party whose members stood for the maintenance of the Corn Laws, but from the early 1840's he began to lose his belief in their desirability. That he himself came from a manufacturing family doubtless helped him to appreciate the case against them. He came to realize that, now that Britain was mainly an industrial country, it could no longer hope to be self-supporting in food. He saw also that the landed classes could not expect to be advantaged at the expense of dearer than necessary food for the growing number of working people. In the spring of 1845 occurred the well-known incident when Peel found himself unable to answer a speech by Cobden in the House of Commons condemning the Corn Laws (no. 1026).

His plan now was to seek to persuade his party during the two years before the next general election that they must support him as a free trader and present themselves to the electorate as a party pledged to repeal the Corn Laws; but he was not to have the time he needed. His plan was ruined by the wet summer of 1845, which produced a bad harvest in England and, accompanied by a blight spreading from America, destroyed three-quarters of the Irish potato crop upon which most of the island's population depended for their food. Ireland could not be fed from England, and the Corn Laws prevented cheap corn being obtained from abroad. Peel could no longer delay. 'Rotten potatoes have done it all,' declared Wellington. 'They put Peel in his damned fright; but he had already been convinced about the rightfulness of repeal.

By October 1845 Peel had resolved it must take place at once. When he told the Cabinet, only Gladstone and Lord Aberdeen would follow him. He delivered his resignation to the Queen, but when Russell failed to form a government, he agreed to resume the premiership, and in the event all the previous ministers except one agreed to serve again under him. He secured the passage of the Bill by 25th. June 1846, but on the same night an Irish measure introduced by the government was defeated, and Peel forthwith resigned.

Though Peel repealed the Corn Laws to avert the threat of famine and revolution, at the same time he took advantage of the situation to make a deliberate attempt to stimulate cost-reducing improvements in British agriculture. In the speech in which he outlined his plans for repeal, he considered schemes for drainage loans and other high productivity measures. His practical interest in agriculture was indicated by the fact that he was a charter-member of the English Agricultural Society founded in 1838, which later became the Royal Agricultural Society of England.

The repeal of the Corn Laws had, in fact little immediate effect upon the condition of farming in the country. The hopes of the abolitionists and the fears of their opponents were seen to be largely groundless for some thirty years. The price of corn in Britain remained almost unchanged during that period because there were not enough foreign growers to invade the market at a competitive price. Not until the development of the American and Canadian wheat-growing prairies in the 1870's did the did the farmers have to face severe competition from large-scale imports of cheaper foreign food. The immediate importance of repeal was political rather than economic. With the disappearance of the Corn Laws, the last outpost of protectionism, the way was now open for the country to adopt the policy of free trade which was to be unchallenged for the rest of the century.

543. Archbald Prentice, History of the Anti-Corn Law League (2 vols., Cash, 1853)

544. D.G. Barnes, A History of the English Corn Laws, 1660-1846 (Bell, 1930)

545. George L. Mosse, 'The Anti- Corn Law League,1844-1946,' Economic History Review, vols. XVII-XVIII (1947-1948), pp. 307-316

546. G.S.R. Kitson Clark, 'The Repeal of the Corn Laws and the Politics of the 'Forties,' Economic History Review, Second Series, vol. IV, no. 1 (1951), pp. 1-13

547. G.S.R. Kitson Clark, 'The Electorate and the Repeal of the Corn Laws,' Transactions of the Royal Historical Society, Fifth Series, vol. I (1951), pp. 109-126

548. Lucy Brown, The Board of Trade and the Free-Trade Movement, 1830-1842 (OUP, 1958)

549. N. McCord, The Anti-Corn Law League, 1838-1846 (Allen & Unwin, 1958)

550. A.H. Imlah, 'The Fall of Protection in Britain,' D.E. Lie & G.E. Mcreynolds (eds.), Essays in Honor of George Hubbar Blakeslee (Clark Univ. Pubn., Worcester, Mass., 1959)

551. Mary Lawson-Tancred, 'The Anti- Corn Law League and the Corn Law Crisis of 1846,' Historical Journal, vol. III (1960), pp. 274-281

552. K.B. Nowlan, The Politics of Repeal (Routledge,1965)

553. S. Fairlie, 'The Nineteenth-Century Corn Laws
     Reconsidered,' Economic History Review, Second Series,
     vol. XVIII, (1965), pp. 26-34

554. D.C. Moore, 'The Corn Laws and High Farming, Economic
     History Review, Second Series, vol. XVIII, (1965),
     pp. 544-561

555. W.O. Aydelotte, 'The Country Gentlemen and the Repeal of
     The Corn Laws,' English Historical Review, vol. XXIV
     (1967), pp. 19-38

556. R. Stewart, The Politics of Protection (CUP, 1971)

557. Travis L. Crosby, English Farmers and the Politics of
     Protection (Harvester Press, 1971)

THE PEELITES

The Peelites first appeared as the famous 112 Conservatives who
voted for Peel in favour of the repeal of the Corn Laws and
adhered to him over the Irish Coercion Bill. Many of them did so
out of loyalty to him rather than because they believed in free
trade. Mostly administrators and business men, they included the
great majority of the Conservative Cabinet Ministers and party
officials.

The repeal of the Corn Laws and the collapse of Peel's
government in June 1846 threw British politics into uncertainty.
Peel now gave his supported the Whig government in its
continuation of Whig liberal policies without showing any sign
of being willing to assume office in it. At the same time, he
occupied an ambivalent position in the Conservative party. He
had no intention of retiring from his place in the Conservative
party, but nevertheless he persistently refused to consider
giving it any active leadership again or support any attempts to
secure the restoration of Conservative unity. Though the
Peelites remained loyal to him, he would not recognize them as
having any political coherance or consider taking any part in
organizing them into an effective party (see no. 1170).

Yet, despite their uncertain position, many of them,
including nearly all their ex-ministers, were returned to
Parliament in the general election of 1847 and sat as a group
under Sidney Herbert and Gladstone on the opposition side of the
House of Commons; but they suffered, as Gladstone and Goulborn
recognized, from a serious lack of leadership and cohesion (see
nos. 1166, 1168). This was still their position in 1850 when Peel
died, which further affected their circumstances.

Their numbers were now reduced to less than seventy in the
House of Commons, and they still lacked a recognized leader. They
enjoyed little popular support in the country; they were like a
group of army officers without either a general or a battalion.
The Times observed, 'Their present difficulty is that they are
not a party; they have not its ties; they have not its facilities;
they have not its obligations,' and it concluded that they were
kept together by 'a mere historical connexion with Sir Robert
Peel.'

Moreover, their indecisiveness contributed to persistence of
the general situation of political instability in Parliament and
the country. They would not support the Liberal government of

Lord John Russell from July 1846 to February 1852. Traditional past antipathies strongly remained, and Peel's death had, in fact, made them more independent of the Liberals.

Nor would they assist the Conservative government of Lord Derby which succeeded it. He would not make any promise about what action he would take about the Corn Laws, and they could not tolerate Disraeli as Chancellor of the Exchequer. Forming a government without the inclusion of the Peelites meant that, apart from Derby and Disraeli, the ministers were undistinguished and unknown, and it became known as the 'Who? Who? Cabinet' from the aged Duke of Wellington's repeated question when the list of their names was read out to him. Disraeli recognized that free trade had to be maintained. 'Protection is not only dead,' he said; 'it stinketh.' In his budget he attempted through taxation to compensate agriculture, shipping and the sugar industry, which had particularly been injured by the abandonment of protection, Gladstone attacked the proposal in a scathing speech, which secured the rejection of the budget with the help of the Peelites, who were sympathetically portrayed in the fiction of Trollope (no. 1174)

This led to the downfall of the government before the end of the year after it had been in office for less than ten months. Since it was now apparent that neither a Liberal nor a Conservative administration could function effectively without the co-operation of the Peelites, a coalition government seemed inevitable, and since the Conservatives were losing national support, it would have to be formed by the Liberals and the Peelites. It was equally certain that the Prime Minister would have to be Lord Aberdeen, who had served in ministerial posts under Wellington and Peel, become the leader of the Peelites after Peel's death and brought about the defeat of Derby by joining with the Liberals.

Though the Peelites were now reduced to forty members in the House of Commons, when Aberdeen formed his Cabinet in December 1852, it contained six Peelites, six Liberals and one Radical. This was partly due to their prestige, experience and ability, but also because he wanted to preserve the identity of the Peelites as the upholders of Peel's outlook. He did not wish them merely to be absorbed by the Liberals. In doing this, he hoped to be able to form a ministry with as wide a political support as possible. 'The new government,' he wrote, 'must not be a revival of the old Whig Cabinet with the addition of some Peelites, but should be a liberal Conservative government in the sense of Sir Robert Peel.'

The Peelites did do much to lead the government in the direction of measures of domestic reform and administrative efficiency which were a continuance of Peel's past policies. As Chancellor of the Exchequer, Gladstone carried further the reduction of customs duties in his budget of 1853; and the Peelites were largely responsible for reforming the system of admission into the civil service and the statutes of the University of Oxford. But other important proposals could not be carried out. This Liberal-Peelite coalition, which had been established with such hopeful enthusiasm, was fated to last for little more than two years.

In March 1854 the Crimean War against Russia broke out. Its first year was marked by British reverses and administrative weaknesses. By January 1855 Lord Aberdeen had lost the confidence of the House of Commons and resigned. He was

replaced as Prime Minister by Lord Palmerston, who, was (as
Churchill was to be in May 1940) regarded as capable of being the
war leader who would secure victory. Palmerston had long been
suspected by the Peelites. He had been attacked over the Don
Pacifico affair by Peel himself in what was to be his last speech
in 1850; and they did not think that he was at all sympathetic
with their political outlook. And after a few weeks, their
differences with the new Prime Minister led to their resignation
from the government.

Palmerston secured the defeat of Russia in 1856, and in the
general election he gained a resounding triumph. He had a
majority of eighty-five in the House of Commons, and the Peelites
were reduced to a mere twenty-five of whom the majority were the
former ministers in Peel's last administration. The Times
asserted that this meant that 'the Peelite party is no more;' and
Aberdeen believed 'the amalgamation of Peel's friends with the
Liberal party to have practically taken place.' This, indeed,
had been becoming increasingly likely ever since the Peelites
had joined the coalition government of 1852. It was, however,
delayed, largely because Gladstone, who was becoming recognized
as the leader of the younger Peelites, could not bring himself to
be a colleague of Palmerston. The result was a Conservative
government under Derby in 1858. Gladstone, however, soon changed
his mind, the main reasons being that he believed that the
Liberals supported his financial principles and favoured the
reforms in the franchise which he considered necessary, and he
also sympathised with the nationalist cause in Italy which
Palmerston supported. His action in effect made inevitable the
end of the Peelites as a separate political group; and in June
1859, the leaders of the opposition parties met at Willis's Rooms
in London, agreed to join a government under Palmerston and
defeated Derby's government two days later (see no.656).

This marked the return of an effective two-party system,
which had been in abeyance in British politics since 1846. The
Peelites disappeared as an independent entity, but their ideas
were to inspire the Liberal party during the remainder of the
nineteenth century. As H.C.G. Matthew has said in his
Introduction to The Gladstone Diaries, Gladstone became 'the
codifier, legislator and guardian of the canons of Peelite
finance.' The ascension of the Liberals inevitably involved a
serious set-back for the Conservatives, who took over a decade to
recover from the splitting apart of their party. Not until
Disraeli's victory in the general election of 1874 did they
obtain their first secure majority in the House of Commons since
Peel's time.

558. E. Halévy, A History of the English People   in the
     Nineteenth Century, vol. III, The Triumph of Reform,
     1830-1841, p. 180, n.1, stating that the term 'Liberal'
     became official in 1847.

559. C.H. Stuart, 'The Formation of the Coalition Cabinet of
     1852,' Transactions of the Royal Historical Society, Fifth
     Series, vol. IV (1954), pp. 45-68

560. J.R. Vincent, 'The Parliamentary Dimensions of the
     Crimean War,' Transactions of the Royal Historical
     Society, Fifth Series, vol. XXXI (1981), pp. 37-50

561. J.B. Conacher, 'Peel and the Peelites, 1846-1850,'
     English Historical Review, vol. LXXIII (1958),
     pp. 382-397

562. N. Gash, English Politics: Reaction and Reconstructiojn
     in English Politics, 1832-1852 (Macmillan, 1965)

563. J.B. Conacher, The Aberdeen Coalition, 1852-1855
     (CUP, 1965)

564. J.B. Conacher. The Peelites and the Party System, 1846-
     1852 (David & Charles,Newton Abbot, Devon, 1972)

565. Wilbur D. Jones & Arvel. B. Erickson, The Peelites, 1846-
     1857 (Ohio State University Press, Columbus, Ohio,
         1972)

566. John Vincent, The Formation of the British Liberal Party
     (Pelican Books, 1972)

567. Robert Blake, The Conservative Party from Peel to
     Thatcher - formerly The Conservative Party from Peel
     Churchill (Fontana, 1985)

568. Arvel B. Erickson, 'Edward T. Cardwell: Peelite,'
     Transactions of the American Philosophical Society,
     New Series, vol. IL, pt. 2, Philadelphia (1959)

569. Lady Frances Balfour, The Life of George, Fourth Earl of
     Aberdeen (2 vols., n.d.)

570. Sir Arthur Gordon (Lord Stanmore), The Earl of Aberdeen
     (New York, 1893)

571. Arvel B. Erickson, The Public Career of Sir James Graham
     (Oxford & Cleveland, OUP, 1952)

572. Sir Arthur Gordon (Lord Stanmore), The Life of Henry
     Pelham, Fifth Duke of Newcastle (Sampson Low, 1908)

573. John Morley, The Life of Gladstone (2 vols., Edward
     Lloyd, 1908)

7

Periodicals

574. Albion

575. Apollo

576. Archivium Hibernicum

577. Australian Journal of Politics and History

578. Bulletin of the Institute of Historical Research

579. Canadian Historical Review

580. Economic History Review

581. English Historical Review

582. Historical Journal

583. History Today

584. Institute of Bankers Journal

585. Irish Historical Studies

586. Journal of Ecclesiastical History

587. Journal of Modern History

588. Oregon Historical Quarterly

589. Political Science Quarterly

590. Quarterly Journal of Speech

591. Queen's Quarterly

592. Revue Historique Moderne

593. Tijdschrift voor Geschiedenis

594. Transactions of the American Philosophical Society

595. Transactions of the Royal Historical Society

78   Sir Robert Peel

596. <u>Victorian Studies</u>

597. <u>Westminster Review</u>

598. <u>Yorkshire Archaeological Journal</u>

8

Contemporary Portraits of Peel

Peel's favourite painter was Sir Thomas Lawrence. He collected his pictures and was a pall-bearer at his funeral in 1830. For such an important statesman as Peel, there are surprisingly few portraits of him. In later life he was unwilling to have his picture painted because, some friends and acquaintances believed, he disliked Linnell's portrait of 1838 (no. 614) as inadequate, though they admit that he may have given some authorisation for it.

Also, while a daguerrotype of Wellington survives from this pioneer age of photography, when Peel, soon after his fall from office in 1846, was asked to sit for a companion daguerrotype, which was to be engraved on steel, he refused (The Times, 26th. October 1944). Since this process involved a cumbersome technique and needed considerable skill to produce a good image, he may have considered that the result would also have been inadequate. At any rate, he probably appears to have been the last Prime Minister never to have been photographed.

Descriptive accounts of portraits of Peel are contained in:

599. C.R.L. Fletcher & Emery Walker, Historical Portraits, 1700-1850, pt. II, 1800- 1850, OUP, 1919)

600. R. Osmond, Early Victorian Portraits (2 vols., HMSO, 1973)

601. Kenneth Garlick, Sir Thomas Lawrence (Phaidon, Oxford, 1989)

The following is what is known of the existing portraits of the Peel family:

602. ?Philip Reinagle: Robert 'Parsley' Peel (undated painting)
Formerly at Drayton Manor and now in the possession of Earl Peel.

603. Sir Thomas Lawrence: Sir Robert Peel, first baronet (c. 1825)
Earl Peel

604. There are several paintings that are stated to be portraits by Lawrence of Peel as a boy or as a young man, but these are probably variants of a portrait by him of Ayscoghe Boucherett, Junior (c. 1795). It is very unlikely that Peel sat for Lawrence when he was a boy or a young man.

605. William Owen: Peel aged 23 (1811)
National Portrait Gallery, London

606. Sir Thomas Lawrence: Peel aged 32 (1820)
Earl Peel

607. Sir Thomas Lawrence: Peel aged 37 (1825)
This is probably the best portrait of him.
Earl Peel

608. Sir Thomas Lawrence: Julia, Lady Peel (1824)
The Frick Collection, New York

609. Peter Christopher Wonder: Peel with David Wilkie and Lord Egremont (c. 1826)
National Portrait Gallery, London

610. Arthur Pedrigal: Peel meeting guests at the Manchester Fancy Dress Ball, the culmination of the Manchester Music Festival, 1828.
Salford Art Gallery

611. H.B. (John Doyle), <u>Political Sketches</u>
917 lithograph cartoons issued separately between 1829 and 1851
These probably display the best impression of him during that period - 'the man as he is daily seen' (<u>Westminster Review</u>, vol. XVIII - VI new style - 1838), p. 292.

612. Sir George Hayter: group portrait of the House of Commons, 1833.
Peel features prominently on the Opposition front bench.
National Portrait Gallery, London

613. Sir George Hayter: members of the House of Lords, c. 1835
Only the head of Peel appears in the picture.
National Portrait Gallery, London

614. John Linnell: Peel aged 50 (1838)
Its fuzzy vagueness is perhaps due to it not being painted directly from Peel.
National Portrait Gallery, London
Another version of the picture is owned by Earl Peel.

615. Henry William Pickersgill: Peel aged about 53 (c. 1841)
Its woodenness is perhaps due to the same reason as above, but Lord Liveagh (who originally owned the painting) was told by one of Peel's sons that it was the most lifelike portrait of him that he knew.
National Portrait Gallery, London
A slightly different version of the picture is owned by the Home Office

616. Franz Xavier Winterhalter: Peel aged 56 and the Duke of Wellington (1844)
They sat for it at Queen Victoria's request. It expresses Peel's general expression and attitude.
Her Majesty the Queen

617. Sir George Hayter: Members of the Fine Arts Commission, 1846
National Portrait Gallery, London

9

Caricatures of Peel

618. Mary Dorothy George, <u>Catalogue of Personal and Political Satires Preserved in the Department of Prints and Drawings in the British Museum</u> (HMSO, 1938 - 1947; reprinted 1978)
     The many caricatures of Peel are to be found among those listed and described in vols. III to VI.

619. M.D. George, <u>Hogarth to Cruickshank: Social Change in Graphic Satire</u> (OUP, 1967)

620. The 17,000 prints in the British Museum, from all periods, can be had in microfilm published by Chadwyck-Healey, Ltd., Cambridge, 1978.

621. The Morgan Library of New York possess Sir Robert Peel's collection of political satires contained in twelve folio volumes.

622. H.B. (John Doyle), <u>Political Sketches</u> (1829-1851)
     See no. 610.

623. <u>Punch or the London Charivari</u>, vols. I-X (1841-1950)
     See no. 167

     Further relevant books and articles are:

624. Thomas Wright, <u>Caricature History of the Georges</u> (1868) - first published in two volumes as <u>England under the House of Hanover</u> (1848)

625. Graham Everitt, <u>English Caricaturists and Graphic Humourists of the Ninetenth Century</u> (Swan Sonnerschein, 1893)

626. M.H. Spielman, <u>History of Punch</u> (Cassell, 1895)

627. George Paston (pseudonym of Emily Morse Symonds), <u>Social Caricature in the Eighteenth Century</u> (Methuen, 1905)

628. G.M. Trevelyan (ed.), <u>The Seven Years of William IV, A Reign Cartooned by John Doyle</u> (Longmans, 1952)

629. M.D. George, _English Political Caricature,1793-1832_ (Longmans, 1959)

630. J.B. Jones & Priscilla Shaw, 'Artists and "Suggestions": the _Punch_ Cartoons, 1843-1848,' _Victorian Periodicals Newsletter_, vol. XI (1978),pp. 3-14

10

Places Associated with Peel

631. PEEL FOLD, OSWALDWISTLE

In 1771 Robert Peele, the first of the family to be clearly
identified, bought a two-storeyed yeoman's farmhouse at
Oswaldwistle, a hamlet in East Lancashire. It was then called
Oldham's Cross, but he renamed it Peele Fold, and it became Peel
Fold when his grandson, Robert ('Parsley'), abandoned the final
'e' in the family name. The descendants of William, his eldest
son, still own the house. The first Sir Robert Peel was born there
on 25th. April 1750. There is an illustration of it in CSP, vol.
I, p. 5.

632. CHAMBER HALL, BURY

Soon after his marriage in 1738, the first Sir Robert Peel bought
this farmhouse near to the cotton-printing works at Bury Ground
on the border of the town of Bury. It was situated on the left
bank of the River Irwell directly north of Bury market-place on
low ground at the foot of the flat track of higher ground on
which the old town was built. The house was mostly of stone and
timber, but he took down its front part and rebuilt it in brick.
He did not move into it until this had been completed in January
1788. His son Robert was born the next month in the old part of
the house, ivy-covered and facing a courtyard. The house was
demolished in 1909.
    There is an illustration of the old Chamber Hall in The
Pictorial History of Lancashire (1844), opp. p. 25, and of the
refronted house in B.T. Barton, History of the Borough of
Bury (1874), opp. p. 95.

633. DRAYTON HALL, DRAYTON BASSETT

The old manor house, Drayton Hall, at Drayton Bassett, a village
on the borders of Staffordshire and Warwickshire and a few miles
south of Tamworth,was bought in 1796 by the first Sir Robert
Peel. It was originally a rambling, half-timbered sixteenth-
century structure with low-gabled buildings erected in the
manner of the time around a quadrangle with small rooms and
separate staircases; but when he took possession of it, it had
suffered from neglect, and a large part had been pulled down. He
completely demolished what remaained of the old house and built a
plain, solid, rectangular three-storeyed country mansion.
    This lasted until 1852 when on the death of his father,

the second baronet considered it too small and plain and replaced it by a great new house, which was designed by Sir Robert Smirke in a Jacobean style with broad, short-angle towers, an Italian campanile, balustrades, gables and mullioned windows - a typical example of the eclectic architecture of the period. It was opulent, but it was also comfortable with efficient up-to-date sanitation and heating, which was much appreciated by visitors from old country homes. The park was laid out by William Gilpin, and during the spring and summer, when Peel was in London, his wife sent him violets, strawberries and new potatoes from the gardens. It was his favourite house, and he enjoyed leading there the life of a simple country squire - 'A Day at Tamworth and Drayton - Sir Robert Peel as Landlord,' Morning Chronicle, 8th. June 1844. It was demolished in 1926, and the park is now occupied by a golf course, a small zoo and a steak house with accompanying lounges. A few fragments of the outbuildings and garden ornaments are now all that remain.

There are engravings of Peel Fold and of the two Drayton Halls, built by the Peels, father and son, reproduced in Norman Gash, Peel, opp. p. 195, and a photograph of the later Drayton Hall in CSP, vol III, opp. p. 452.

634. HARROW SCHOOL, MIDDLESEX

Though now engulfed by the growth of suburban London, the village of Harrow-on-the-Hill was, when Peel went there in 1800, still surrounded by the open, flat Middlesex countryside. The School's first brick buildings, completed in 1615, were virtually unchanged. All the classes, numbering together over three hundred boys, were taught in the original single schoolroom, now known as the Fourth Form Room, which still exists with its oak-panelled walls carved with the names of Peel and other former pupils. Peel was assigned to board in the house of Mark Drury, the Headmaster's brother, in the High Street, a red-brick Georginan building now used by the school bookshop.

There are engravings of the School, including an interior scene of the schoolroom showing boys being taught there, in Rudolph Ackermann, History of Harrow School (1816).

635. CHRIST CHURCH, OXFORD

The large and wealthy Christ Church, though it is to all purposes an Oxford college, is technically not one; it is a 'house' attached since Henry VIII's time to Christ Church Cathedral, which serves also as its Chapel. When Peel went there in 1805, the reputation of Cyril Jackson had made it full to overflowing. During his first year, the set of rooms in which he lived were no. 8 on staircase 7 on the east side of the Peckwater Quadrangle that had been built during the eighteenth century round three sides of the old Peckwater Inn, and it is likely that the numbering of these rooms has remained unchanged since then. They were not especially commodious or expensive, and he moved out of them the next year, probably to lodgings in the town, but nothing is known of where he went.

For views of Oxford as known by Peel see Rudolph Ackermann, History of the University of Oxford: Its Colleges, Halls and Public Buildings (2 vols., 1814); Ackermann's Oxford, with notes by H.M. Colvin (OUP, 1954).

636. HOUSE OF COMMONS, WESTMINSTER

When Peel became a Member of Parliament in 1809, the House of Commons met, as it had done since 1547, in St. Stephen's Chapel within the Palace of Westminster, which had been vacated as a royal residence by Henry VIII; the Chapel is now the site of St. Stephen's Hall in the present Houses of Parliament. By Peel's time, the growth of the United Kingdom had needed alterations to be made to the old Chapel. In 1707 Sir Christopher Wren inserted three round-headed windows in the east end (above the Speaker's Chair where the altar had formerly stood), lowered the roof and added galleries for the forty-five Scottish members; and in 1800 James Wyatt made the walls thinner to accommodate the hundred Irish members. In 1834 the Houses of Parliament were largely destroyed by fire, and the Commons met in the old House of Lords until 1847 when their new Chamber (destroyed by enemy action in 1941) was completed.

The picture of the interior of the House of Commons in Rudolph Ackermann & A.C. Pugin, The Microcosm of London, shows it as Peel knew it.

637. 11 LITTLE SCOTLAND YARD, WESTMINSTER

While Peel was Under-Secretary for War and Colonies from 1810 to 1812, Lord Liverpool allowed him the use of this small house for himself. Though a detached building, it was actually part of Fife House, which was Lord Liverpool's town residence. It stood near to the Thames and north of Whitehall Stairs. Peel's house had its own entrance in Little Scotland Yard. The site is now occupied by the headquarters of the Ministry of Defence.

638. SECRETARY'S LODGE, PHOENIX PARK, DUBLIN

As Chief Secretary for Ireland from 1812 to 1818, Peel resided in the Secretary's Lodge in Dublin. It was a low, two-storeyed house, flanked by projecting bow-fronted wings, which had been built during the last quarter of the eighteenth century. It was in a considerable state of neglect when Peel arrived, and he had to undertake extensive repairs, including the strengthening of the drawing-room ceiling by columns in imitation marble. During Victorian times later Chief Secretaries made additions to the building; and it is now the American Embassy.

639. DUBLIN CASTLE

The Castle was the official residence of the Lord-Lieutenant and the seat of government. Between 1730 and 1763 extensive remodelling made it essentially the brick building of to-day. It comprises two courts, and in the upper court were the state apartments, including the offices which Peel had as Chief Secretary.

640. IRISH OFFICE, 18 GREAT QUEEN STREET, WESTMINSTER

The Irish Office was both a place of business and an official residence for the Chief Secretary during the parliamentary session when he was in London. All routine letters between Britain and Ireland passed through the office, and Peel made use of it to obtain parcels of fresh salmon from Ireland.

Sufficient early eighteenth-century houses remain in the street to indicate its appearance during his time.

641. 36 GREAT GEORGE STREET, WESTMINSTER
12 STANHOPE STREET, WESTMINSTER

Though still a bachelor, Peel did not want to reside in the Irish Office, and in January 1813, since he had to move from Little Scotland Yard, he took this house, which belonged to George Vansittart, on a year's lease with an option to purchase. The street was built between 1752 and 1757; its eighteenth-century buildings no longer exist.
At the end of his tenancy of 34 Great George Street, Peel decided to move to 12 Stanhope Street (now Stanhope Gate) off Park Lane. It was built about 1760, and although Peel's house does not survive, several others of the same date do. The street was named after Chesterfield House (now the site of a modern block of flats)   belonging   to   Philip   Stanhope,   fourth   Earl   of Chesterfield.

642. WHITE'S CLUB, 37-38 ST.JAMES'S STREET, WESTMINSTER

In December 1813 Peel was elected to White's Club, the oldest and grandest of the gentlemen's clubs in St. James's, the buildings of which had been rebuilt in 1788 in their present form with the exception of the bow-window added in 1811. Since the late eighteenth century, the Club had become Conservative in the composition of its members, but mainly social again after the formation of the Carlton Club in 1832 (see no. 651). In 1814 White's Club had a membership of 500 and a long waiting list. That Peel was elected so readily indicated the importance he was gaining in the Conservative party.

643. APSLEY HOUSE, PICCADILLY, LONDON

The Duke of Wellington acquired this house, built by Robert Adam in 1778, and made it his permanent London home after leaving the army and entering politics. He faced the brick walls with Bath stone and added the Corinthian portico and the west wing, including the Waterloo Gallery (named from the Waterloo Banquets he held there annually on the anniversary of the battle with his senior officers who had fought there), to the designs of Benjamin Wyatt. Peel took part in several important political discussions in the house, including one of several days in January 1828 which resulted in Wellington forming a government with Peel as Home Secretary and when the new Cabinet for the first time dined together there, Lord Ellenborough observed that 'the courtesy was that of men who had just fought a duel.' Since 1952 the house has been open to the public as the Wellington Museum.

644. CLUNY CASTLE, LAGGAN, INVERNESS-SHIRE

After his resignation in 1818 from his Irish post, Peel took a six weeks summer holiday in the Highlands of Scotland with his brother William and some friends. He rented Cluny Castle, a classical castellated villa built in 1805 as the the seat of Cluny MacPherson, the chief of the Clan MacPherson, lying on the River Spey and among the mountains of Badenoch. Peel brought his own cook with him to serve up each evening the game they shot during the day. The main building remains as in Peel's time except for two additions - a Queen Anne porch in 1891 and a north-western wing in 1908.

645. MARESFIELD PARK, EAST SUSSEX

In January 1819 Peel was introduced to Lady Frances Shelley at a house-party she gave at Maresfield Park, a high-chimneyed, gabled brick house near Uckfield, the seat of her husband, Sir John Shelley. He had inherited it in 1814 and spent £70,000 on additions to it. Two sketches of the house are reproduced in Richard Edgcumbe, The Diary of Lady Frances Shelley, 1787-1873 (2 vols., John Murray, vol. I, pp. 68, 220).

She and Peel met again several times in London, but speculation about their relationship disappeared with Peel's marriage. He rented the house for a holiday with his family in 1827, while Lady Shelley was abroad convalescing after an illness. He was there when, on the death of Canning, he had to come to London for the events which led to the formation of Wellington's government (see no. 856). The elaborate entrance arch into the park and parts of the house remain, but the ornamental grounds with their classic statuary have become a housing estate.

646. 45 SEYMOUR STREET, ST. MARYLEBONE

Built about 1769, this was the home of Julia Floyd's widowed mother in the drawing-room of which she and Peel were married on 8th. June 1820. The site of the house is now occupied by an office block, but some eighteenth-century houses remain opposite.

647. 4 WHITEHALL GARDENS, WESTMINSTER

With a wife and growing family, Peel needed a house that was larger than his residence in Stanhope Street and was nearer Parliament and the government offices. In 1823 he bought from the Crown the lease of one of a row of old houses known as Whitehall Gardens on the Thames between Pembroke House and Montague House and behind the Banqueting House of the former royal Palace of Whitehall. The old house was pulled down and a new one designed for Peel by Sir Robert Smirke. Sixty feet wide, it comprised three storeys over a basement. On the ground floor were the hall, library , dining-room and waiting-room; and on the next floor two drawing-rooms and the gallery extending the full length of the house. Since the Victoria Embankment was not built until 1870, the small garden at the back of the house went down to the River.

The Survey of London, vol. XIII (1930), pp. 198-203, contains Peel's plan and an illustration of the house. Its site is now occupied by the headquarters of the Ministry of Defence.

648. ROYAL PAVILION, BRIGHTON, EAST SUSSEX

Prince George built this marine palace at Brighton, eventually giving it the oriental character it now has. When he became King as George IV, he still stayed there quite frequenyly, and Peel when he was Home Secretary, sometimes went there to confer

with him. The King supported him in reforming the criminal code
and liked to be able to persuade him to use the royal prerogative
of mercy in capital cases. In the middle of one night,when Peel
was staying in the Pavilion, he summoned him to his presence to
ask him to pardon a criminal about to be executed. When Peel
agreed, he excitedly kissed him and then, noticing the poor
quality of the Home Secretary's dressing-gown, suddenly
exclaimed, 'Peel, where <u>did</u> you get that dressing-gown? I'll
show you what a dressing-gown should be'' And he made Peel put on
one of his own - Roger Fulford, <u>George IV</u> (1949). p. 224.

649. 18 & 32 SUSSEX SQUARE, BRIGHTON, EAST SUSSEX

At other times Peel went to Brighton, particularly during the
parliamentary summer recess, when he frequently stayed at one or
the other of these two houses. Number 18 was occupied by his
sister, Mary, who married George Dawson, M.P., and number 32 by
his youngest brother, Lawrence, whose wife, Lady Jane Peel, was a
daughter of the fourth Duke of Rutland. The fifty houses of
Sussex Square were built in 1828, and are part of Kemp Town, the
estate for wealthy middle-class residents designed by Thomas
Reed Kemp.

650. SCOTLAND YARD, WESTMINSTER

In 1820 a row of houses was built in Whitehall Place, a small
street between Whitehall and the Thames. In 1829 Peel acquired
one of these houses -number 28 - which was vacant, to be the
headquarters of his newly-established police force, where it
remained until 1890. The house backed on to a parallel street,
Great Scotland Yard, and was approached through an archway from
the street,so that the headquarters became known as 'Scotland
Yard.' The site of the house, which is marked by a blue plaque, is
occupied by the Ministry of Agriculture and Fisheries.

651. CARLTON CLUB, WESTMINSTER

The general election of 1832 returned only 179 Tories out of a
total membership of the House of Commons of 658. Peel and
Wellington supported a plan to establish a social club which
would also be a meeting-place for Tories where they could engage
in political activity and immediately oppose the Reform Bill. It
was founded in March 1832 with some 500 members, mostly peers and
Members of Parliament. It took its name from its first premises
in no. 2 Carlton House Terrace; it moved in 1835 to a specially
designed building by Sir Robert Smirke in Pall Mall. This was
replaced by a new building in 1854 on the same site, which was
bombed in 1940. The Corn Law crisis bitterly divided the Club as
also did the defeat of Lord Derby's government in 1852, when
Gladstone was insulted by angry Tory members, though he did not
actually resign until 1860. The Club now occupies a building in
St. James's Street, and its site in Pall Mall (between the Reform
Club and the Royal Automobile Club) is occupied by a modern
office block.

652. APETHORPE HALL, NORTHAMPTONSHIRE

In January 1833 Peel went to a house-party held at Apethorpe Hall
by its owner,the Earl of Westmorland. He wrote from there to

his wife, 'The house is exactly like a small college in Oxford.' It had, in fact, been the home of Sir Walter Mildmay (1520?-1589) and served as a model for his foundation of Emmanuel College, Cambridge, in 1585. Peel's room there looked into the quadrangle and was so draughty that his candle was blown out when he went to bed, and he could not relight it.

653. 10 DOWNING STREET, WESTMINSTER

Sir George Downing in about 1680 built this street of plain brick terraced houses. The Crown acquired number 10 in 1732, and George II offered it as a gift to Sir Robert Walpole, who accepted it only on the condition that it should become the official residence of the First Lord of the Treasury (later called the Prime MInister), which it has been ever since. Interior alteration to the building were carried out by William Kent in 1735, and the house is now substantially as it was in Peel's time, including the Cabinet Room, where on 2nd. December 1845 he told his ministers that he intended to repeal the Corn Laws. A complete silence followed, broken finally by Lord Stanley's announcement of his immediate resignation. Like most nineteenth-century Prime Ministers, Peel preferred to live in his own town house, and let number 10 out. For part of the time he allocated it to his Private Secretary, Edward Drummond, whose death it brought about (see no. 654).

654. DRUMMOND'S BANK, CHARING CROSS, WESTMINSTER

Andrew Drummond, a Scottish goldsmith, established a bank in LOndon, which he moved to its present site in 1760. After his death the bank remained in the family to which Edward Drummond, Peel's Private Secretary, was related. On 20th. January 1842, after he had done business at the Bank, he was shot outside and died five days later. His assailant mistook him for Peel, having seen him entering and leaving number 10 Downing Street (see no. 653).

655.EILEAN AIGAS, KILMORACK, INVERNESS-SHIRE

In August 1849 Peel took his last Scottish holiday. He went with his wife and youngest child, Eliza, to a house called Eilean Aigas, which he rented from Lord Lovat. The house, built in 1839 and probably now still as much as Peel knew it except for wings added to the back in 1858, stands on an oval, rocky island, about three-quarters of a mile long and 1½ miles round, on a deep gorge of an expansion of the River Beauly. By then Peel's fondness for shooting had declined, and he enjoyed the grandeur and quietness of the country, staying there until the middle of October.

656. WILLIS'S ROOMS, 50 PALL MALL, WESTMINSTER

On 6th.June 1859 the leaders of the parliamentary opposition met in Willis's Rooms. Palmerston, Russell and Bright were on the platform, and Sidney Herbert was also there. Palmerston and Russell said they were willing to serve under each other, and Bright gave his support to both, thereby establishing a new Liberal party. Willis's Rooms had been Almack's Club founded been Almack's Club in 1762 for drinking and gambling. It was now aristocratic and exclusive, managed by a group of leading

Whig ladies, most of whom, however, were involved in irregular sexual unions, some with Palmerston himself. The site is now occupied by a modern office block.

11

Peel's Life and Career

EDUCATION AND ENTRY INTO POLITICS (1788-1822)

657. Jane Haworth, MS. Memoir of the Family of Peel from the
     Year 1600 (1836), BL. Add. MSS. 40160
658. Jonathan Peel, A Memoir of the Genealogy of the Peels
     (n.d.), pp. 20-29
659. LP, pp. 6-8
660. B.T. Barton, History of the Borough of Bury (1874)
661. W.A. Abram, History of Blackburn (Toulmin, Blackburn,
     1877), pp. 204-206, 212-224
662. S.D. Chapman, 'The Peels in the Early English Cotton
     Industry,' Business History, vol. XI (1969), pp. 61-89
     The History of the Peel Family.

663. T. Briggs, Pedigree of...Sir Robert Peel (Blackburn,
     1885)
664. W.A. Abram, op. cit., p. 18
665. LP, p. 24
666. J. Peel, op. cit., p. 93
667, NG1, pp. 20-22
     Robert ('Parsley') Peel.

668. T. Briggs, op. cit.
669. CSP, vol. I, p. 5
     'Sir Robert Peel, the first baronet, on 'Parsley' Peel -
     'My father moved in a confined sphere and employed his talents in
     improving the cotton-trade. He had neither wish nor opportunity
     of making himself acquainted with his native country or society
     far removed from his native county of Lancashire.... The only
     record of my father is to be found in the memory of his surviving
     friends.'

670. T. Briggs, op. cit.
671. CSP, vol. I, p. 5
672. Richard Davies, A Memoir of Sir Robert Peel (1803)
673. Gentlemen's Magazine vol. I, pp. 556-557
     Sir Robert Peel (First Baronet).

674. Journal of John Wesley, 27th. July 1787
     'I was invited to breakfast at Bury by Mr. Peel, a calico-
     printer, who a few years ago began with five hundred pounds and is
     now supposed to have gained fifty thousand pounds. Oh, what a
     miracle if he lose not his soul.'

675. PH, vol. XXXIV, pp. 478ff.
676. R. Davies, op. cit., pp. 31n, 33
677. Victoria County History of Lancaster (1908), vol.II,
        p. 396
678. Letters of the First Earl of Dudley to the Bishop of
        Llandaff (1841), p. 344
     The First Baronet's cotton manufactories.

679. Parliamentary Papers, 1816, No. III, (Children in
        Manufactories, pp. 132ff.
680. AW, pp. 5-6
681. S.J. Chapman, Lancashire Cotton Industry (Manchester,
        1904), pp. 85-90
     Conditions in the manufactories.

682. Gentleman's Magazine, no. 5, New Series, 1st. May 1866
683. NG1, p. 32n
684. A.F. Robbins, Notes and Queries, Seventh Series,
        vol. XII, p. 61
     Birth of Robert Peel - 681 & 682: his place of birth;
     685: the 'dedication to the country' story.

686. G.M. Young, Victorian England,Portrait of an Age (OUP,
        1936), p. 15
     'Old Sir Robert Peel trained his son to repeat every Sunday
the discourse (sermon) he had just heard, a practice to which he
owed his astonishing recollection of his opponents' arguments
and something, perhaps, of the unction of his own replies.' (See
also CSP, vol. I, p. 10; NG1, p. 36).

687. NG1, pp.41-47
688. LP, pp. 48ff.
689. CSP, vol. I, chap. i
690. Lord Dalling. Sir Robert Peel (1874), p. 7 (LD)
     Peel at Harrow School.

691. LP, p. 7
692. NG1, pp. 44-45
     Lord Byron on Peel at Harrow - 'Peel was my form-fellow, and we
were both at the top of our remove. There were always great hopes
of Peel amongst us, masters and scholars, and he has not
disappointed them. As a scholar he was greatly my superior, as a
declaimer and actor I was reckoned at least his equal. As a
schoolboy out of school I was always in scrapes and he never;   in
school he always knew his lesson and I rarely; but when I knew it,
I knew it nearly as well. In general information, history,etc.,
I think I was his superior, as well as of most boys of my
standing.'

693. W. Harvey, Sir Robert Peel (1850), p. 28
694. NG1, pp. 49-59
695. Charles Edward Mallet, A History of the University of
        Oxford (3 vols.,OUP, 1924-1927), vol. III, pp. 167-169
696. W.J. Hiscock, A Christ Church Miscellany (OUP, 1946)
697. J.F.A. Mason, Christ Church and Reform (OUP, 1970)
698. Hugh Trevor-Roper, Christ Church, Oxford (OUP, 2nd. ed.,
        1973)
     Peel at Oxford.

699. Bl, Add. MSS. 4065, f.5
700. NG1, pp.57-58
     George Dawson to Mark Drury, 19th. November 1808 on
     Peel's examination success at Oxford.

701. Spencer Perceval to George III, 24th. January 1810,
     Windsor MSS
702. Spencer Walpole, Life of the Rt. Hon. Spencer Perceval
     (2 vols.,1874), vol. II, p. 58n.
703. Earl of Bessborough (ed.), Lady Bessborough and Her...
     Circle (Bell, 1940), p. 202
704. K.G. Feiling, The Second Tory Party, 1714-1832
     (Macmillan, 1938), p. 262
705. NG1, pp. 68-70
     Peel and the Reply to the King's Speech, 23rd. January
     1810.

706. Sir Herbert Maxwell (ed.), The Creevey Papers (John
     Murray, 2 vols., 1904), vol. I, p. 122
     23rd. January 1810 - 'Peel ... made a capital figure for a
     first speech. I think it was a prepared speech, but it was   a
     most produceable Pittish performance, both in matter and in
     manner.'
        Creevey's comment on Peel's speech.

707. Public Record Office, C.O. 324/134; W.O.
     6/29-30, 6/122-123
708. NG1, p. 74
     Peel as Under-Secretary for War and Colonies, 1810-1812

709. Wellington's Supplementary Despatches, vol. VII, p. 87
710. NG1, p. 87
     Liverpool to Wellington, 19th. August 1812 - 'I have had
     therefore no resource but to bring forward the most promising of
     the young men, and the fate of the government in the House of
     Commons in another session will depend very much on their
     exertiions. I should be most happy if I could see a second Pitt
     arise among them and would most willingly resign the government
     into his hands, for I am fully aware of the importance of the
     minister being, if possible, in the House of Commons.'

711. R. Dunlop, Ireland from the Earliest Times to the
     Present Day (Humphrey Milford,1922)
712. E. Curtis, A History of Ireland (Methuen, 1936)
713. H. Shearman, Anglo-Irish Relations (Methuen, 1948)
714. J. Carty, Ireland, A Documentary Record, 1607-1921
     (Fallon, Dublin, 3 vols., 1949-1950)
715. K.H. Connell, The Population of Ireland, 1750-1845
     (Cassell, 1950)
716. R.B. McDowell, Public Opinion and Government Policy in
     Ireland, 1801-1846 (Faber, 1952)
717. H. Shearman, Ireland Since the Close of the Middle Ages
     (Harrap, 1955)
718. M. Hayden & J. Moonan, A Short History of the Irish
     People (Longmans, 1960)

719. J.C. Beckett, <u>The Making of Modern Ireland, 1603-1923</u>
     (Faber & Faber, 1966)
     Ireland during Peel's time.

720, C. Maxwell, <u>Dublin Under the Georges</u> (Harrap, 1946)
721. J.C. Curwen, <u>Observations ... on Ireland</u> (2 vols.,
     1818), vol. II, pp. 103-132
     Dublin during Peel's time.

722. NG1, pp. 177ff
723. Gilen Booker, 'Robert Peel and the Peace Preservation
     Force,' <u>Journal of Modern History</u>, Vol. XXXIII (1961),
     pp. 363-373
724, Tadhg Ceallaigh, 'Peel and Police Reform in Ireland,'
     <u>Studia Hibernica</u>, vol. VI (1966), pp. 25-48
     The Police Preservation Force, 1814

725. CSP, vol. I, p. 145
     Peel to William Gregory, 24th. June 1814 - 'I said the (Peace
Preservation) Bill was not meant to meet any temporary
emergency, but was rendered necessary by the past state of
Ireland for the last fifty years and by the probable state of it
for the next five hundred.'

726. Robert Carl Shipsey, 'Problems of Irish Patronage during
     the Chief Secretaryship of Robert Peel, 1812-1811
     <u>Historical Journal</u>, vol. X (1967), pp. 41-56
727. Robert Carl Shipsey, <u>Robert Peel's Irish Policy,
     1812-1846</u> (Garland, 1987)
728. Oliver McDonagh, 'Politics 1830-1845,' W.E. Vaughan
     (ed.), <u>A New History of Ireland</u>, vol. V, <u>Ireland
     under the Union, i, 1807-1870</u> (OUP, 1989), pp. 169-192
     Peel's connection with Ireland.

729. BL, Add. MSS., 40222, ff. 5, 20, 64; 40223, f. 142;
     40280, f. 117
730. NG1, pp. 105-106
     Peel became M.P. for Chippenham.

731. BL, Add. MSS., 40266, ff. 295ff
732. National Library, Dublin, Richmond Papers, 269ff
733. <u>Report on the Manuscripts of Earl Bathurst</u> (Hist. Mss.
     Commission, 1923), pp. 385-386
734. <u>Dublin Evening Post</u>, 2nd. September - 5th. October 1815
735. J. O'Connell, <u>Life and Speeches of Daniel O'Connell</u>
     (2 vols., 1846), vol. II, pp. 217ff
736. Shaw Eversley, <u>Peel and O'Connell</u> (1887), p. 310
737. AR, pp. 46-47, 94ff, 107ff, 117, 124, 161, 166, 175
738. NG1, pp. 162-167
     Daniel O'Connell's quarrel with Peel.

739. CCD, vol. I, p. 75
740. Bernard Pool (ed.), <u>Croker Papers</u> (Batsford, 1967),
     p. 32
     Peel to Croker, Dublin Castle, 8th. August 1815 - 'I had a
passage of thirty-three hours from Holyhead - two nights and a
day. Wretched beyond description - a strong N.W. by W., if such a
wind blows. I mean westerly, with just enough inclination to
the north to make it a completely foul wind. The packet was

full of passengers. The men were all sick, and the women and children thought that they were going to the bottom....'

741. CSP, vol. I, pp. 247-250
742. NG1, pp. 205-210
     Peel's R.C. Emancipation speech, 9th. May 1817.

743. BL, Add. MSS. 40625,f.248; 40266, ff. 148-151, 176;
     40293, ff. 95-96; 40342, f. 207
744. CSP, vol. I, pp. 250-251
745. Lord Colchester (ed.), Diary and Correspondence of
     Charles Abbot, Lord Colchester (3 vols., 1861), vol.
     II, pp. 328, 374, 610; vol. III, pp. 3-6
746. H. Twiss,Life of Lord Chancellor Eldon (3 vol,. 1844),
     vol. II, p. 295
747. Report on the Manuscripts of Earl Bathurst, Liverpool
     to Bathurst, 31st. May 1817 (Hist. Mss. Commission,
     1923), p. 434
748. Edward Marshall, Diocesan History of Oxford (SPCK,
     1882,pp. 174-175
749. GN1, pp. 211ff.
     The Oxford University Election of 1817.

750. Sir Charles Petrie, George Canning (Eyre &
     Spottiswoode, 2nd. ed., 1946), p. 137
     Wellesley Pole to Sir Charles Bagot, June 1817 - 'You must have forgotten English politics to suppose that Canning would have a chance for Oxford. Nothing but a violent, unrelenting Protestant would be tolerated by that sage University, and Mr. Peel was invited (I believe without any intrigue of his) and returned unanimously in consequence of his speech, which was a very good one, on the Catholic question last session.'

751. CSP, vol. I, p. 256
     Lord Palmerston to Peel, 19th. August 1817 - 'Could you tell me ... whether you think there is any probability of a contest for the county of Sligo at the next election? I could at the present make from 280 to 290 voters by giving leases to tenants who are now holding at will. If there is any chance of them being of use next year, I will do so forthwith and register them in time. If not, I should perhaps postpone giving them 21 year leases till matters look a little more propitious to the payment of rents.'

752. CSP, vol. I, passim
753. CCD, vol. I, pp. 46ff
754. Mr. Gregory's Letter Box, passim
755. Diary of Lady Frances Shelley, vol. I, pp. 16ff
756. G. Kitson Clark, Peel and the Conservative Party,
     pp. 6-12
     Peel's work in Ireland.

757. SRP, vol. I, p. 91
     Peel's parliamentary speech supporting his father's Factory Bill, 19th. February 1818 - 'A great change has taken place in the manner of conducting that (cotton) manufactory since that period (1802). Before the application of steam, it was necessary to select situations where falls of water could be had; these situations were frequently mountainous, and its population

thin; and the children were obtained as apprentices from large towns; but now these manufactories were in populous neighbourhoods. The individual in question (his father), finding that in his own establishments abuses had taken place and were kept from his knowledge by the overseer and learning that the same abuses took place in other manufactories, gave proof of his sincere wish to remedy this evil.'

758. CSP, vol. I, pp. 237, 286
759. CCD, vol. II, p. 116
760. Memoirs of Plumer Ward, vol. II, p. 48
761. State Papers Office, Dublin, Irish Privy Council
     Minutes
762. NG1, pp.235-236
     Peel's resignation from the Irish Secretaryship, 1818.

763. Croker Papers (ed. Pool), p. 41
     Peel to Croker, 1818 - 'A fortnight hence I shall be free as air - free from ten thousand engagements which I cannot fulfil; free from the anxiety of having more to do than it is possible to do well; free from the acknowledgements of that gratitude which consists in a lively sense of future favours; free from the necessity of abstaining from private intimacy that will certainly interfere with public duty....'

764, AR, pp. 61ff
765. GN1, pp. 260ff
766. Kirsty McLeod, The Wives of Downing Street (Collins,
     1976), pp. 44-63
     Peel's Marriage, 8th. June 1820.

767. Foreign Office, Stratford-Canning Papers, vol. VIII
768. Sir Charles Webster, The Foreign Policy of Castlereagh
     (Bell, 2 vols., 2nd. ed., 1963), vol. II, App. G, pp.
     581-582)
     Joseph Planta to Stratford Canning, 9th. January 1821 - 'After his (Canning's) withdrawal, Peel was sounded but held off, chiefly he said from family considerations - he has married a young wife - partly from not feeling so strongly as the Government do about the Liturgy - but not at all on account of the office offered to him.... Upon the whole he did not wish to take office at present. This we consider somewhat shabby.'

HOME SECRETARY (1822-1830)

769. The Sentences of All the Prisoners in the Old Bailey,
     which Commenced on Wednesday, 1th. September 1822.
'Death - Richard Mitford, alias Captain Stracey for forgery; William Adams for cutting and maiming; William Callaghue for returning from transportation; Samuel Wilson, Isaac Knight and James Simpson for horse-stealing; Samuel Greenwood, John Bridgeman, Robert Ramsey, Thomas Gordon, William Milton and John Levy for highway robbery; Thomas Hayes, William Williams, Joseph Williams, Francis Waddell, Mary Gyngell, Daniel Coltre, John Brown, Walter Blanchard, Alexander Brown, Frank Pardon, William Corbett, alias Watson, Charles Robinson and Joseph Mackarell for stealing in dwelling houses; William Reading for burglary, Edmund Mustoe, James Gardner, William Bright and George Vergenton for robbing near the highway; and John Partier, John

Roberts and Stephen Tool for burglary.'
    An extract from a contemporary broadsheet illustrating the
capital crimes of the time.

770. Francis Sheppard, London 1808-1870: The Infernal Wen
        (Secker & Warburg, 1871), p. 57
771. Trevor May, An Economic and Social History of Britain,
        1760-1970 (Longmans, 1987), p. 132
    Report of the Select Committee on Police of the Metropolis,
1822 - 'It is difficult to reconcile an effective system of
police with that perfect freedom of action and exemption from
interference, which are the great privileges and blessings of
society in this country;and Your Committee think that the
forfeiture of such advantages would be too great a sacrifice for
improvements in police or facilities in detection of crime,
however desirable in themselves if abstractly considered.'

772. John Prebble, The King's Jaunt, George IV in Scotland,
        1822 (Collins, 1928), passim
773. NG1, pp. 276-277, 301ff
    Peel and George IV's visit to Scotland, August 1822.

774. SRP, vol. II, pp. 239-240
    Peel on the reform of the penal code,30th. April 1823 - 'It was
peculiarly incumbent upon those who advocated the necessity of
mitigating the severity of the penal code in respect to capital
punishments to beware of rendering   such an experiment
impracticable by narrowing too much the scale of minor
punishments. For his own part, he had always been friendly to the
punishment of whipping when exercised within salutary
limits.... Solitary confinement was, in his opinion, a much more
rigorous punishment, and one which was much more likely to break
the spirit than a moderate whipping. There were some instances of
offences in young delinquents of a nature so flagrant that no
other punishment seemed to have any effect upon them.'

775. NG1, pp. 344-345, 381-351, 619
776. AR, pp. 74ff
777. Henry Pelling,A History of British Trade Unionism
        (Penguin Books,1973)
    Peel and the Combination Laws, 1824-1825.

778. NG1, pp. 413-414
779. W. Hinde, George Canning (Longmans, 1973), p. 397
    Sir Francis Burdett's Roman Catholic Emancipation Bill
passed by the Commons, but defeated by the Lords.

780. Morning Herald, 19th. April 1825
    'On Hyde Park walls at Knightsbridge there is written, "Peel
for ever! No Cardinal Burdett!"'

781. R.L. Shiell (ed. M.W. Savage), Sketches Legal and
        Political (2 vols., 1855, vol. II,, pp. 39ff
782. NG1, pp. 665-666
    A description of Peel in the House of Commons, c. 1825 - 'I do
not like his physionomy as an orator. He has a handsome face, but
it is suffused with a smile of sleek self-complacency, which it
is impossible to witness without distaste. He has also a

trick of closing his eyes, which may arise from their weakness, but which has some thing mental in its expression; and however innocent he may be of all offensive purpose, is indicative of a superciliousness and contempt.'

783. H. Maxwell, Creevey Papers, vol. II, p. 100
     3rd. May 1826 - 'That prig Peel seems as deeply bitten by "liberality," in every way but in the Catholic question, as any of his fellows.'

784. BL, Add. MSS. 4032, ff. 322-328; 40343, ff. 2-5, 14, 22, 24; 40305, ff. 265, 273, 283, 309; 3815, f.192
785. CSP, vol. I, pp. 438ff
786. GN1, pp. 406-408
     Elevation of Charles Lloyd to the Bishopric of Oxford, 1827.

787. GM, 12th. April 1827
788. Diary of Henry Hobhouse, p. 128
789. NG2, pp. 431-441
790. Peter Dixon, Canning, pp. 278-279
     Peel's refusal to serve with Canning, 1827.

791. CSP, vol. I, p. 465
     Canning to Peel, 15th. April 1827 - 'Adieu,my dear Peel. I will relieve you as soon as I can from the labours of your office, which is the one I find most difficult to fill - no wonder, after such a predecessor.'

792. CSP, vol. I, p. 466
     Peel to Canning, 17th. April 1827 - 'I do not consider that my objections to remain in office resolve themselves merely into a point of honour. The grounds on which I decline office are public grounds, clear and intelligible,I think, to every man who has marked the course which I have pursued in Parliament on the Catholic question, and who understands the nature and functions of the office which I have filled.'

793. CSP, vol. II, p. 17
     Peel to Bishop Lloyd, 26th. August 1827 - 'The proposal of office to me was in effect saying to me, "Govern Ireland without support, discountenanced by all that is influential in the Government, and when we have discredited you, we will remove you"'

794. MC, vol. I, pp. 11-12
795. CSP, vol. II, p. 27
796. NG1, p. 452
     Wellington to Peel, 9th. January 1828 - 'I have declined to make myself the head of the Government unless upon discussion with my friends it should appear desirable , and excepting Lord Lyndhurst, who it must be understood is in office, everything is open to all mankind, excepting one person (Lord Grey). I have sent for nobody else, nor shall I see anybody till you come.'

797. Gordon Huelin, King's College, London, 1828-1978
     (University of London King's College, 1978), pp.
     1-3, 5,9

798. H.M. Bates, <u>Somerset House</u> (Frederick Muller, 1967),
     pp. 159-160
799. NG1, p. 581
   Peel and King's College,London.

800. Sir Charles Grant Robertson (ed.),<u>Select Statutes,
     Cases and Documents, 1660-1832</u> (Methuen, New Issue,
     1935), pp. 312-316
   Act to Repeal the Test and Corporation Acts , 9 Geo. IV,
Cap. 17, 1828 - 'Be it therefore enacted,...That so much and such
parts of the said several Acts (e.g., the Corporation Act, 1661,
and the first Test Act,1673, relating to Protestant Dissenters
and public offices) ... as require the person or persons in the
said Acts respectively described to take or receive the
Sacrament of the Lord's Supper according to the rites and usage
of the Church of England ... or to impose on any such person or
persons any penalty, forfeiture, incapacity or disability
whatsoever for or by reason of any neglect or omission to take or
receive the said Sacrament ... shall, from and immediately after
the passing of this Act, be, and the same are, hereby
repealed.'

801. MC, vol. I, pp. 114-15
802. NG1, p. 522
   Vasey Fitzgerald (the defeated candidate) to Peel, 5th. July
1828,on the result of the Clare election - 'Such a scene as we
have had! Such a tremendous prospect as it opens to us.... The
organisation exhibited is so complete and so formidable that no
man can contemplate without alarm what is to follow in this
wretched country.'

803. <u>Croker Papers</u> (ed. Pool), p. 122
   From his Diary, 2nd.February 1829 - 'Saw Peel, to whom I felt
it to be due to say that the greatest surprise of the public was
not so much the concession to the Catholics, as his consenting to
be the mover of it....'

804. Grant Robertson, <u>Statutes and Documents</u>, pp. 317-327
   Roman Catholic Emancipation Act,10 Geo. IV, Cap. 7, 1829 -
'Whereas by various Acts of Parliament certain restraints and
disabilities are imposed on the Roman Catholic subjects of his
Majesty, to which other subjects of his Majesty are not liable;
and whereas it is expedient that such restraints and
disabilities shall be from henceforth discontinued: and whereas
by various Acts certain oaths and declarations, commonly called
the declaration against transubstantiation, and the declaration
against transubstantiation and the invocation of saints and the
sacrifice of the mass, as practised in the Church of Rome, are or
may be required to be taken, made and subscribed by the subjects
of his Majesty, as qualifications for sitting and voting in
Parliament, and for the enjoyment of certain offices, franchises
and civil rights: Be it enacted,... That from and after the
commencement of this Act all such parts of the said Acts as
require the said declarations,... as a qualification for sitting
and voting in Parliament, or for the exercise or enjoyment of any
office, franchise or civil right, be and the same are ... hereby
repealed.'

805. MC, vol. I, pp. 310ff
806. Journal of Mrs. Arbuthnot,vol. II, p. 239
807. Norman Gash, Oxoniensia, vol. IV (1939), pp. 162ff
808. NG1, pp. 506ff, 658
   The Oxford University Election of 1829.

809. John Skinner, Journal of a Somerset Rector, 1803-1834
     (OUP, 1894), p. 381
   '22nd. February 1829. The places in the Oxford (coach) were
all engaged on account of the contest about the re-election of
Mr. Peel. I hope to my heart he will be thrown out as a
turncoat.'

810. SRP, vol. I, pp. 698-762
   Peel's speeches on Roman Catholic Emancipation, 5th.-3oth.
March 1829.

811. Christopher Hibbert, George IV (Penguin Books, 1976),
     pp. 752-753
   The King at Ascot races, 1829 - 'He gave a bad reception to all
the friends of government who went to his stand, and said to
Mr.Peel that he should soon have expected to see a pig in church
as him at a race! Mr. Peel was invited to dine at the Lodge, but he
pretended he had no clothes and refused to go.'

812. Sunday Times, 20th. September 1829
   'The whole corps of policemen are to assemble on 26th. at the
Foundling Hospital, to be inspected previous to the commencement
of their neighbours.'

813. CSP, vol. ii, p. 128
   Peel to Wellington, 5th. November 1829 - 'I want to teach
people that liberty does not consist in having your house robbed
by organized gangs of thieves and in leaving the principal
streets of London in the nightly possession of drunken women and
vagabonds.'

814. NG1, pp. 627-629
815. Journal of Mrs. Arbuthnot, p. 355
   Death of Peel's father, 3rd. May 1830.

816. Peel to his Wife, 11th. May 1830, Peel MSS
817. NG1, pp. 628-629
   The provisions of his father's will - 'All the lands in
Staffordshire, Warwickshire and Lancashire left to the eldest
son and his descendants, and such an arrangement made with
respect to money as gives upon the whole (land and money
included) four times the amount to the eldest son of that sum
which each younger son has. You may be quite at ease. In short,
the will is what I always told you I thought it would be.'

818. BL, Add. MSS, 40323, f. 124
819. R.W. Jefferey (ed.), Dyott's Diary, vol. II, p. 170
820. CCD, vol. II, p. 629
821. NG1, p. 629
822. Christopher Hibbert, The Court at Windsor (Longmans Green,
     Peel's meeting with George IV at Windsor, 17th. May 1830.
     1964), p. 175

REFORM AND THE NEW CONSERVATIVES (1830-1835)

823. A. Aspinall (ed.),Three Early Nineteenth-Century
     Diaries (Williams & Norgate, 1952), p. 43
   Lord Ellenborough, 28th. January 1831 - 'Peel does think
chiefly of himself and has not the manner or the character to
become a popular leader of a party. He likes to do all himself and
does not defend his friends when they speak.'

824. GM, 2nd. March 1831
   'What everybody enquires is, what line Peel will take, and
though each party is confident of success in this question, it is
thought to depend mainly upon the course he adopts and the
sentiments he expresses.'

825. CSP, vol. II, p. 177
826. J.R.M. Butler, The Passing of the Great Reform Bill
     (FRank Cass, 2nd. ed.,1964), pp. 199-200
827. Michael Brock, The Great Reform Act (Hutchinson, 1973),
     p. 163.
828. NG2, pp. 11-13
   Peel's first speech on the Reform Bill, 3rd. March 1831.

829. GM, 28th. March 1831
   'I have never heard anything like the complaints of Peel - of
his coldness, incommunicativeness and deficiency in all the
qualities requisite for a leader, particularly at such a time.
There is nobody else or he would be deserted for any man who had
talents enough to take a prominent part, so much does he disgust
his adherants.'

830. GM, 29th. April 1831
   'I hear renewed complaints of Peel, of his selfish, cold,
calculating, cowardly policy; that we are indebted principally
for our present condition I have no doubt - to his obstinancy and
to his conduct in the atholic question, for his opposition and
then to his support of it. Opposing all and every sort of Reform
totis virilis while he dared, now he makes a deathbed profession
of acquiesence in something which should be more moderate than
this.'

831. The Times, 2nd. August 1831
   Because of Tory opposition to the Reform Bill, the crowd
booed Peel when he was taking his part in the procession led by
King William IV across the new London bridge at its opening.

832. A. Aspinall, Three Nineteenth-Century Diaries (1952),
     pp. 118-119
   Le Marchant, 19th. August 1831 - 'One of the most aimiable
traits in Peel's life was his attachment to (Charles) Lloyd. He
perhaps was his only confidant, in short, his father confessor.
Lloyd was a sensible man and of essential service to him....
Lloyd used to say that Peel when a young man at Oxford always did
what he was bid and never minded work.'

833. SPR, vol. II, p. 433
834. NG2, p. 26
   On the Third Reform Bill, 17th. December 1831 - 'I am
satisfied with the constitution under which I have lived

hitherto, which I believe is adapted to the wants and habits of the people.... I will continue my opposition to the last, believing as I do, that this is the first step, not directly to revolution, but to a series of changes which will affect the property and totally change the character of the mixed constitution of this country. I will oppose it to the last, convinced that though my opposition will be unavailing, it will not be fruitless, because the opposition now made will oppose a bar to further concessions hereafter.... On this ground I take my stand, not opposed to a well-considered reform of any of our institutions which need reform, but opposed to this reform.'

835. CSP, vol. II, pp. 201-202
836. NG2, p. 38
   Peel to Lord Harrowby, February 1832 - 'Why have we been struggling against the Reform Bill in the House of Commons? Not in the hope of resisting its final success in that House, but because we look beyond the Bill.... We want to make the "descensus" as "difficilis" as we can to teach young, inexperienced men charged with the trust of government that, though they may be backed by popular clamour, they shall not override on the first springtide of excitement every barrier and breakwater raised against popular impulses.... These are salutary sufferings, that may I trust make people hereafter distinguish between the amendment and the overturning of their institutions.'

837. Lord Sudley (ed.), The Lieven-Palmerston Correspondence, 1828-1856 (John Murray, 1943), p. 35
   Princess Lieven to Lady Cowper, 27th. January 1832 - Yesterday I had a conversation with the Duke of Wellington. He is utterly opposed to the (Reform) Bill; he intends to vote against it in every particular, and he foresees the end of the world after the Bill is passed. Peel, who was also dining with us yesterday, is strongly opposed to it himself, but he does not foresee the future as W. foresees it. He does not think that everything is lost, but even thinks that it will still be quite possible to have a tolerable Government in England. There you have the difference between forty and seventy.'

838. Disraeli Letters, p. 192
   Disraeli to Sarah D'Israeli, 24th. March 1832 - 'Yesterday I dined at (Lord) Eliot's - a male party consisting of eight. I sat between Peel and Herries.... Peel was most gracious. He is a very great man indeed, and they all seem afraid of him.... I could easily conceive that he could be very disagreeable, but yesterday he was in a most condescending mood and unbent with becoming haughtiness.'

839. Sir William Fraser, Disraeli and his Day (1891), p. 187
840. Duke of Wellington (ed.), Despatches,Correspondence and Memoranda of the Duke of Wellington, 1819-1832 (8 vols., 1867-1880, vol. VIII, pp. 30-32
841. CCD, vol. II, pp. 153-169
842. A. Aspinall (ed.), Three Nineteenth-Century Diaries (1952), pp. 247-258
843. GM, 12th., 14th., 17th. May 1832

844. GN2, pp. 29-33
     The Days of May (7th.-14th. May 1832)

845. Croker Papers (ed. Pool), pp.153-154
     Peel to Croker, 12th. May 1832 - 'I don't believe that one of
the greatest calamities that could befall the country would be
that utter want of confidence in the declarations of public men
which must follow the adoption of the Bill of Reform by me as a
Minister of the Crown. It is not a repetition of the Catholic
question. I was then in office. I had advised the concession as a
minister. I should now assume office for the purpose of carrying
the measure to which, up to the last moment, I have been
inveterately opposed as a revolutionary measure.'

846. A. Aspinall (ed), Three Nineteenth-Century Diaries
     (1952), p. 253
     Littleton, 14th. May 1832 - 'His (Peel's) game and intention
clearly is to watch the tide and not to embark until he thinks it
favourable. His is a mere practical head, with great dexterity in
treating subjects before him, but it is not a master mind that can
create circumstances or control them when they come; and his
prudence is always more conspicuous than his generosity or
courage. His talent is eminently for turning things to his own
account.'

847. CSP, vol. II, pp. 212-213
     Peel to Goulburn, 3rd. January 1833 - 'I presume the chief
object of that party which is called Conservative, whatever its
number may be, will be to resist Radicalism, to prevent those
further encroachments of democratic influence, which will be
attempted - probably successfully attempted - as the natural
consequence of the triumph already achieved.... The best
position the Government could assume would be that of moderation
between opposite extremes of Ultra-Toryism and Radicalism. We
should appear to the greatest advantage in defending the
Government, whenever the Government espoused our principles, as
I apprehend they must do if they mean to maintain the cause of
authority and order.'

848. SPR, vol. II, pp. 612-613
849. Paul Adelman, Peel and the Conservative Party,
     pp. 102-103
     Peel's acceptance of the Reform Bill, 7th.February 1833 -
'The King's government had abstained from all unseemly triumph
in the King's Speech respecting the measure of reform. He would
profit by the example and would say nothing upon that head; but
consider that question as finally and irrevocably disposed of.
He was now determined to look forward to the future alone and,
considering the constitution as it existed, to take his hand on
main and essential matters - to join in resisting every attempt
at new measures, which could not be stirred without unsettling
the public mind and endangering public prosperity.'

850. GM, 14th.February 1833
     'He (Peel) is one of those contradictory characters,
containing in it so much of good and evil, that it is difficult to
strike an accurate balance between the two,and the acts of his
political   life   are   of   a   corresponding   description,of
questionable utility and merit, though always marked by great

measures of   ability.'

851. <u>Croker Papers</u> (ed. Pool), pp. 167-168
Peel to Croker, 5th. March 1833 - 'the question is not, Can you turn out a Government? but, Can you keep in any Government and stave off confusion?
What are we doing at this moment? We are making the Reform Bill work; we are falsifying our own predictions, which would be realised but for our own active interference; we are protecting the authors of the evil from the work of their own hands.'

852. <u>The Times</u>, 25th. June 1833
853. G.B.A.M. Finlayson, <u>England in the Eighteen-Thirties,</u>
      <u>Decade of Reform</u> (Edward Arnold, 1969)
'The most active spring of election bribery and villany everywhere is known to be the Corporation system.... The fact is that Parliamentary Reform, if it were not to include corporation reform likelwise, would have been literally a dead letter, except in so far as the county representation be concerned.'

854. GM, 13th. November 1833
'He (Peel) is very agreeable in society, it is a toss up whether he talks or not, but if he thaws and is in good humour and spirits, he is lively, entertaining and abounding in anecdotes, which he tells extremely well.'

855. GM, 22nd. February 1834
On Peel's oratory - 'His great merit consists in his judgement, tact and discretion, his facilitude, promptitude, thorough knowledge of the assembly he addresses, familiarity with the details of every sort of Parliamentary business and the great command he has over himself.'

856. BL, Add. MSS 40302ff
857. BL, Ellenborough Papers, 19th. November 1834
858. MC, vol. II, pp. 14ff
859. L.C. Sanders, <u>Melbourne Papers</u> (1889), pp. 219ff
860. GM, 16th.-19th. November 1834
861. David Cecil, <u>Lord M</u> (Grey Arrow, 1962), pp. 102-104
      Resignation of Melbourne, 14th. November 1834.

862. CSP, vol. II, pp. 251-257
863. Gustavo Dalgas, <u>Lecture in Commemoration of Sir James</u>
      <u>Hudson</u> (Privately Printed, 1887)
864. W.M. Torrens, <u>Memoirs of Viscount Melbourne</u> (Macmillan,
      1890), pp. 316-317
865. Sir Algernon West, <u>Recollections, 1832-1886</u> (Nelson,
      n.d.), p.50
866. MC, vol. II, pp.24-32
867. BL, Ellenborough Papers, 5th. & 9th. December 1834
868. Surrey Record Office, Goulburn Papers, Memorandum Book
      on Travel Expense, Italian Visit, 1834
869. <u>Portion of a Journal Kept by T. Raikes, Esq., 1831-1847</u>
      (4 vols., 1856-1858), vol. I, pp.308-310

870. Emma Sophia, Countess Brownlow, <u>The Eve of Victorianism,</u>
      <u>1802-1834</u> (John Murray, 1940), pp.190-195
871. NG2, pp. 81-83
Hudson's journey to Rome (15th.-25th. November 1834 and

Peel's return to London (26th. November-8th. December 1834).

872. BL, Add. MSS. 40404, ff. 266, 340; 40318, f. 7; 40309,
      f. 380
873. PRO, Ellenborough Papers, 9th.-10th. December 1834
874. GM, 29th. November 1834
875. MC, vol. II, pp. 28-35
876. NG2, p. 86
    Peel's appointment as Prime Minister, 9th.December 1834

877. B.T. Barton, Borough of Bury, p. 83
    Peel's Address to the Electors of Tamworth on becoming Prime
Minister, 1834 - 'With respect to the Reform Bill itself, I will
repeat now the declaration which I made when I entered the House
of Commons as a Member of the Reformed Parliament, that I
consider the Reform Bill a final and irrevocable settlement of a
great constitutional question - a settlement which no friend to
the peace and welfare of this country would attempt to disturb,
either by direct or by insiduous means.'

878. BL, Add. MSS. 40405, ff. 202, 325, 327
879. PRO, Ellenborough Papers, 13th., 14th., 16th.-19th.
      December 1834
880. GM, 20th. December 1834
881. History of The Times (5 vols., 1935-1952), vol. I,
      pp. 340-344
882. NG2, pp. 93-99, 107, 125, 130, 236
    The Tamworth Manifesto, 18th. December 1834.

883. J.R. Thursfield, Peel (Macmillan, 1891), pp. 136-142
884. Norman Gash (ed.), The Age of Peel, pp. 76-77
    The Text of the Manifesto.

885. Journal of Thomas Raikes, p. 312
    22nd. December 1834 - 'It (the Tamworth Manifesto) is a manly
and sensible document calculated to inspire confidence in the
country; expressing readiness to reform real abuses and defects,
without seeking for a false popularity by adopting every
fleeting popular impression of the day and promising the instant
redress of any thing which any one may call an abuse.'

886. BL, Add. MSS. 40, 406; 122,200; 40, 408; 162, 171, 1731;
      40, 412; 17
887. The Times, 24th. December 1834
888. GM, 24th. December 1834
889. MC, vol. II, p. 52
890. G. Kitson Clark, Peel and the Conservative Party,
      p. 215
891. NG2, pp. 97-98
    Peel's Mansion House Speech, 23rd. December 1834.

892. Lieven-Palmerston Correspondence,p. 76
    Princess Lieven to Lady Cowper,6th. February 1835 - 'There is
no doubt that the individuals who form the Government are men of
talent, industry and experience. Peel has all these qualities in
a marked degree, and even his most ardent opponents cannot fail
to respect him.'

893. GM, 21st. February 1835
'In all his (Peel's) ways, his dress, his manner, he looks more like a dapper shop-keeper then a Prime Minister. He eats violently and eats cream and jellies with his knife.'

894. Carola Oman, The Gascoyne Heiress, The Life and Diaries of Frances Mary Gascoyne Cecil, 1802-1839 (Hodder & Stoughton, 1968), p. 158
21st. March 1835 - 'Peel rises in reputation every day; he is so immeasurably superior to all his opponents that they shrink to nothing before him and own themselves that he is the only man who can now govern the country with any prospect of success. I regard him as a Dieu donné, as is raised up by special Providence for the salvation of the country from civil dissensions, as the Duke (of Wellington) was from foreign conquest.'

895. SRP, vol. III, p. 86
Peel on the Bill for a Royal Charter for London University, 26th. March 1835 - 'I do feel that the position of that portion of his Majesty's subjects who do not conform to the Church of England, and who in consequence of their not submitting to certain religious tests are excluded from the Universities, is deserving of attention. It is a ground of just complaint, and their claim to academical honours is not fairly met.... I myself have no objection to some provision being made that should accord to Protestant Dissenters, who are excluded from the Universities, the power of acquiring academical distinctions.'

896. Carola Oman, op. cit., p. 172
2nd. April 1835 6 'I asked him (Wellington) if he thought Lady Peel had any influence over her husband. "No, she is not a clever woman. Peel did not wish to marry a clever woman."'

897. Gervase Huxley, Lady Elizabeth and the Grosvenors, Life in a Whig Family, 1822-1839 (OUP, 1965), p. 109
'Lady Elizabeth Grosvenor to her Mother, April 1835 - 'As to Sir Robert Peel, he deserves all possible gratitude for what he has done, and I heartily wish he will still be preserved to do still more with fairer opportunities. He is the only person in whom one can feel real confidence, and with one feels that honour and talents go together, and that he is unshackled, unprejudiced and unguided by any party and set of people.'

898. BL, 40318, f. 100
899. CSP, vol. II, p. 349
900. NG2, p. 192
Graham to Peel, 8th.August 1835 - 'In my retirement I shall constantly remember the generous kindness which you have shown me on every occasion, and, if you will allow me the expression, I trust we shall always continue friends. I do not believe there now exists between us one shade of difference of opinion on public matters, and my confidence in you is such, founded on personal regard and respect, that my inclination will be strong to prefer your judgement to my own.'

LEADER OF THE OPPOSITION (1835-1841)

901. James Fenimore Cooper, Gleanings in Europe: England
     (1837-1838), p. 152
   'If there is a word between persuasive and coaxing, I would
select it as a word that best describes the manner of Mr. Peel.
The latter would do him great injustice, as it wants his dignity
and argument and force; and the former would ... do injustice to
the truth.'

902. Staffordshire Advertiser, 6th. January 1838
   'Monday last the new school, built at the expense of Sir
Robert Peel, at Tamworth, was opened. It is built in a chaste
Gothic style of architecture. The scholars, to the number of
about 60, proceeded in order with their master from the old
school to the new one, where they were addressed by the right
hon. baronet in a neat appropriate speech; and three of the best
scholars received from his hand that which he declared to be the
best gift they could receive - a Bible. After prayer had been
offered by the rev. vicar, the children were regaled with roast-
beef and plum-pudding. We were glad to see the right hon. baronet
restored to health, taking part with such evident feeling in the
opening of the school, which owes its erection and support solely
to his bounty, and is one of the many strong proofs given of the
interest he takes in the real welfare of the town and
neighbourhood.'

903. Lieven-Palmerston Correspondence, p. 144
   Lady Cowper to Princess Lieven, 13th. February 1838 - 'The
young Tories are one by one emancipating themselves and treat
the Great Captain (Wellington) like an old woman and Peel like an
ignoramus. They would like to have another Leader in the House of
Commons of more decided views.'

904. George Peel, The Work of Sir Robert Peel, p. 26
   The Comte de Jarnac in 1838 - 'In a vast library crowded with
Parliamentary documents, Sir Robert Peel was seated at those
labours which absorbed his life. Through the long windows of
Whitehall Gardens one could see, so far as the thick and yellow
mists of the old city would allow it, the vast surface of the
Thames crowded with numberless vessels....'

905. John Morley, Life of Richard Cobden, p. 150
   Peel in the House of Commons, 18th. March 1839 - 'I have no
hesitation in saying that unless the existence of the Corn Law
can be shown to be consistent, not only with the prosperity of
agriculture and the maintenance of the landlord's interest, but
also with the protection and the maintenance of the general
interests of the country and especially with the improvement of
the condition of the labouring classes, the Corn Law is
practically at an end.'

906. Sir George Otto Trevelyan, Life and Letters of Lord
     Macaulay (Longmans, Green, 1890), p. 540, n. 1
   '2nd. April 1839, I (Macaulay) dined at (Sir Robert) Inglis's
and met Peel. He was pleasant enough; not a brilliant talker, but
conversible and easy with a little turn in private, as in public,
to egotism.'

907. LV, vol. I, p.159
   Victoria to Melbourne, 8th. May 1839 - 'He (Peel) is such a
cold, odd man she can't make out what he means.... The Queen don't
like his manner after - oh! how different, how dreadfully
different, to that frank, open, natural and most kind warm manner
of Lord Melbourne.'

908. Royal Academy General Assembly Minutes, vol. IV, p. 318
909. Sidney C. Hutchison, The History of the Royal Academy,
      1768-1968 (Chapman & Hall, 1968), p. 106
   Peel's support for the Royal Academy to be free of government
control, 1739 - 'I had the greatest satisfaction therefore in
bearing my sincere Testimony on a late occasion to the Merits and
Public Services of the Royal Academy, and considering the
Independence and free Action of the Institution to be essential
Instruments of its success, I shall always be disposed to claim
for its protection from needless or vexatious Interference.'

910. LV, vol. I, pp. 154-175
911. GM, 10th.-19th. May 1839
912. CCD, vol. II, pp. 341-343
913. Viscount Esher (ed.), The Girlhood of Queen Victoria
      (John Murray, 2 vols.,1912), vol. II, pp. 159-177
914. CSP, vol. II, pp. 388-407
915. Holland House Diaries, pp. 397-402
916. E. Hodder, Life of the Seventh Earl of Shaftesbury
      (1890), pp. 130-132
917. C.S.Parker, Life and Letters of Sir James Graham,
      (John Murray, 2 vols., 1907), vol. I, p. 281
918. Elizabeth Longford, Victoria R.I. (Pan Books, 1964),
      pp. 138-143
919. Dorothy Marshall, The Life and Times of Victoria
      (Weidenfeld & Nicolson, 1972), pp. 53-57
920. NG2, pp. 220-227
921. Alison Plowden, The Young Victoria (Methuen, 1967), pp.
      189-190, 191-192
922. Stanley Weintraub, Victoria, Biography of a Queen (Unwin
      Hyman, 1978), pp.122-123, 153-154
   The Bedchamber Incident, 1839.

923. Queen Victoria's Journal, Royal Archives, Windsor
      Castle
   9th. May 1839 - 'Soon after this, Sir Robert (Peel) said, "Now
about the Ladies," upon which I said I could not give up any of my
Ladies and never had imagined such a thing. He asked me if I meant
to retain all. "All," I said. "The Mistress of the Robes and the
Ladies of the Bedchamber?" he asked, to which I replied they were
of more consequence than the others, and that I could not
consent, and that it had never been done before. He said I was a
Queen Regnant, and that made the difference. "Not here," I said -
and I maintained my right.

924. Croker Papers (ed. Pool), p. 180
   Peel to Croker, 1839 - 'Could it be tolerated that a Queen
might appoint a Mistress of the Robes, without reference to her
minister, whom her minister might know to be perfectly unfit to
be about the person of the Queen.'

925. <u>Standard</u>, 10th. May 1839
'We have heard that the attempt to form the administration, under Sir R. Peel, has for the present failed; <u>not upon</u> any public principle whatever in which her Majesty's sentiments and those of her advisers <u>differed</u>, but merely arising out of the fact, that her Majesty refused to part with <u>some</u> of the ladies of her household.... We say nothing at present as to the public feeling of the conduct of the female clique at the Palace, who, by their misconduct, have, in the Hastings correspondence,* already done their royal mistress such unmerited and almost irreparable mischief.... Will the country submit to being governed by a female camarilla at the Palace?'
* Lady Flora Hastings, a Lady in Waiting, was wrongly accused by the Queen of being pregnant.

926. <u>Globe</u>, 10th. May 1839
'We stated yesterday that the Queen had refused to part with the ladies of her household. This point Sir Robert Peel required should be yielded, and upon her Majesty's firm determination not to part with her personal friends, and to have forced upon her constant society those with whom she had no sympathy, Sir Robert Peel resigned the task of forming an administration....
In this her Majesty has shown herself a worthy scion of the line of Brunswick; and in her determination she will be supported by the country, should it be necessary to make an appeal to its opinion. The party who so long ran riot over the liberties of the people, have dared to attempt to ride rough-shod over the Sovereign, and have been unhorsed by a Queen ere they got fixed in the saddle.'

927. <u>Croker Papers</u> (ed. Pool), 10th. May 1839
928. Tresham Lever, <u>The Life and Times of Sir Robert Peel</u>
     (Allen & Unwin, 1942), p. 184
Croker to the King of Hanover - 'Her Majesty's ball last night was, I am told, rather dull, though she herself seemed in high spirits, as if she were pleased at retaining her ministers. She has a great concert on the 13th., but to both, as I hear, the invitations have been on a very exclusive principle - no Tories being invited who could be on any pretence left out.'

929. F.P.G.Guizot, <u>Memoirs of Sir Robert Peel</u> (1857),
     pp. 83-84
Peel told Guizot, 1840 - 'There is too much suffering and too much perplexity in the condition of the working classes; it is a disgrace as well as a danger to our civilisation; it is absolutely necessary to render the condition less hard and less precarious.'

930. BL, Gladstone Papers, 44819, 50
931. Richard Shannon, <u>Gladstone</u> (2. vols., Hamish Hamilton,
     1982), vol. I, p. 55
W.E. Gladstone on Peel, 1840 - 'There is a manifest and peculiar adaptation in Peel's mind to the age in which he lives and to its exigencies and to the position he holds as a public man. What the ultimate and general effect of his policy may be is a question too subtle and remote for one strongly to presume upon.'

932. William Harris, <u>Caroline Fox</u> (Constable, 1944). p. 226
     Anti-Slavery Meeting, Exeter Hall, London, 13th. June 1840 -
'Sir Robert Peel's demeanour was calm, dignified and
statesmanlike; the expression of his face I did not like, it was
so very supercilious. He was received with shouts of applause,
and truly it is a fine thing to have him enlisted in the
enterprise.'

933. <u>Lieven-Palmerston Correspondence</u>, p. 83
     Lady Palmerston to Princess Lieven, 28th. January 1841 -
'Peel courted French popularity and spoke for effect (in the
House of Commons), so I am not surprised that his speech was well
received in Paris. But it made a bad impression with his Party,
and many of his followers criticised it on the ground that it was
neither English nor sincere. He has annoyed his party in other
ways too, particularly by a popular speech which he made to a
Literary Society in Tamworth, and which was more Radical then
Tory in sentiment.'

934. LV, vol. I, p. 260
     Lord John Russell to Queen Victoria, 6th. March 1841 - 'Sir
Robert Peel made a remarkable speech. Adverting to our present
state of affairs with the United States, he said that much as he
disliked war, yet if the honour or interests of the country
required it, he should sink all internal differences and give his
best support to the Government of his country.'

935. <u>The Times</u>, 1st. May 1841
     'A prodigious excitement was produced in the House of Commons
at 5 o'clock yesterday afternoon by a notice from Lord John
Russell that about Whitsuntide he should move a committee for the
revision of the Corn Laws. This announcement was followed by
repeated outbursts of exaltation on the one side and indignation
on the other.'

936. Royal Archives, Windsor, Y 44/27-44 (Anson Memoranda)
937. BL, Add. MSS. 40303, ff. 257-285
938. CSP, vol. II, pp. 455-458
939. LV, vol. I, pp. 268-274
940. NG2, pp. 259-261
     Queen Victoria's negotiations with Peel, May 1841.

941. Lord Rosebery, <u>Sir Robert Peel</u>, p. 23
942. Tresham Lever, <u>Life and Times of Sir Robert Peel</u>,
     pp. 306-307
     Peel's comment on the Budget of Melbourne's Government,
18th. May 1841 - 'Can there be a more lamentable picture than that
of a Chancellor of the Exchequer seated on an empty chest, by the
pool of a bottomless deficiency, fishing for a budget? I won't
bite: the right honourable gentleman shall return home with his
pannier as empty as his chest.'

943. PRO, Broadlands Papers, SHA/PD/4
     Lord Ashley's Diary, 24th. July 1841 - 'He (Peel) has
abundance of human honesty and not much of Divine faith; he will
never do a dishonourable thing, he will be ashamed of doing a
religious one.'

944. Tamworth Election: Sir Robert Peel's Speech on Nomination Day, 28th. June 1841
945. Speech by the Rt. Hon. Sir Robert Peel, etc, 28th. July 1841
946. The Times, 27th.July 1841
947. B. Kemp, 'The General Election of 1841,' History XXI (1952), pp. 82-91
948. NG2, pp. 265-266
949. BL, Add. MSS. 40485, f. 323 (Comservative gains and losses)
    General Election of 1841.

950. GM, 11th. July 1841
    The reasons for the Conservative victory in 1841 - 'The Whigs complain bitterly of the apathy and indifference that have prevailed, and cannot recover from their surprise that their promises of cheap bread and cheap sugar have not proved more attractive. But they do not comprehend the real cause of this apathy. It is true that there has not been any violent Tory reaction, because there has been no great topics on which enthusiasm could fasten, but there has been a revival of Conservative influence, which has been gradually increasing for some time, and together with it a continually decreasing confidence in the Government.'

951. Lieven-Palmerston Correspondence, pp. 217-218
    Lady Palmerston to Princess Lieven, 6th. August 1841 - 'People are very scornful about his (Peel's) Tamworth speech - he gives a dinner in that little town on purpose to have an opportunity to explain his ideas - and then he explains nothing - he only makes a rather few heavy jokes about doctors who unwisely vaunt their remedies before they have a reputation - with the result that his dinner has given him the name of Quack Doctor and Sir Rhubarb Bill - a pitiable situation.

PRIME MINISTER (1841-1846)

952. NG2, pp. 259-262, 290ff, 629, 645, 670ff, 682, 687, 695
953. Roger Fulford, The Prince Consort (Macmillan, 1949), pp. 106-110, 112, 116
954. Speeches of the Prince Consort (Murray, 1862), pp. 121-122
    Peel's relations with Prince Albert.

955. Seventh Duke of Wellington (ed.), Wellington and his Friends (1963), p. 166
    Wellington, 1841 - 'It is very curious that Sir Robert Peel should have the reputation of being entirely ignorant on foreign affairs. They say that Palmerston has very little consideration for him, and that Foreign Ministers have no confidence in him.'

956. CSP, vol. II, pp. 486-489
957. AR, pp. 290-292
958. Robert Blake, Disraeli (Methuen,1969),pp. 164-165
959. Mollie Hardwick, Mrs. Dizzy (Cassell, 1872), pp. 123-124

960. Stanley Weintraub, <u>Disraeli, A Biography</u> (Hamish
     Hamilton, 1993), pp. 199-200, 254-255
   Disraeli's request, supported by his wife, to Peel for
office, and Peel's refusal, September 1841.

961. National Library of Scotland, Ellice MSS
962. G.B.A.M. Finlayson, <u>England in the Eighteen Thirties</u>
     (1969), pp. 101-102
   Joseph Parkes, 16th. September 1841 - 'I plainly see that the
Anti-Corn Law question is the fanaticism of the day. If Peel
staves off the Question - and he cannot practically settle it
without shivering his "Conservatives" to pieces - he will be
agitated to death.... The agitation of the fanaticism of the day
has only commenced. If not yielded to, it will again assault the
representative system. I see the storm brewing in the talk of
Cobden & Co. They are the Tom Attwoods of 1831-32. The outdoor men
have always scattered the Tories and always will.'

963. <u>Journal of Thomas Raikes</u>, p. 179
   9th. October 1841 - 'I am glad to learn from the best
authority that Sir R. Peel begins to feel that he is gradually
gaining influence with the Queen; and her manner is certainly
become far more gracious towards him than could have been
expected from the untoward circumstance under which he has been
presented to her notice.'

964. The Earl of Bessborough, <u>The Diaries of Lady Charlotte
     Guest, 1833-1852</u> (John Murray, 1950), p. 129
   '9th. February 1842. The debate on the Corn Laws opened this
evening. Sir Robert Peel announced his new plan as to the duties,
and the Tories, I believe, were almost as much discontented with
what he proposed as the Whigs.

965. <u>The Times</u>, 10th. February 1842
   'More than the usual amount of interest was evinced yesterday
evening, both in and out of the House, to hear the rest of Sir
Robert Peel's exposition of the intentions of the Government
with reference to the Corn Laws.... No discussion followed the
Premier's speech, and none was anticipated. Lord J. Russell
merely requested that some return which Sir R. Peel alluded to be
laid upon the table, and an adjournment was on the eve of being
proposed when Mr. Cobden, looking exceedingly lachrymose, rose
from his seat for the purpose, as it was generally thought, of
inflicting upon the House one of his stereotyped speeches, but as
it was clearly evident to the hon. member that his own friends
were not disposed to listen patiently to a long harangue, he had
the good sense to bottle up his indignation for a future
occasion.'

966. LV, vol. I, p. 382
967. Roger Fulford, <u>The Prince Consort</u>, p. 109
   Peel to Prince Albert, 15th. February 1842 - 'Sir, when I had
the honour of last seeing your Royal Highness at Windsor Castle,
I stated to your Royal Highness that it would give me great
satisfaction to have the opportunity from time to time of
apprizing your Royal Highness of the legislative measures in
contemplation of Her Majesty's servants and of explaining in
detail any matters in which your Royal Highness might wish for
information.

968. Diaries of Lady Charlotte Guest, p. 130
   '16th. February 1842. At length Sir Robert Peel wound up the
debate. I liked his speaking exceedingly. His speech was good,
though a very subtle one. The plain English of it was , 'What can
I say? If I say one thing this party will attack me, and if I
assert the contrary, the other party will take me up."
Nevertheless, he crept out of his dilemma very well, if not
ingenuously.'

969. The Times, 20th. February 1842
   'We do not impute to Mr. Cobden an attempt to murder; but we do
impute - we cannot avoid imputing - to him this - that with his
eyes open, knowing fully the threatening consequences to Sir
Robert Peel's life of popular odium, ... he feels no scruple at
recklessly and increasingly labouring to direct that odium
personally and individually on the Minister whose life has been
once already attempted.'

970. John Morley, Life of Richard Cobden, p. 31
   Richard Cobden to his brother, Frederick Cobden, 28th.
February 1842 - 'The Tories have not liked the debate. Peel fears
that he has not come out of it well. He looks dissatisfied with
himself.'

971. AR, pp. 226-230
972. NG2, pp. 138-220
973. GM. 11th.March 1842
   Peel's first Free Trade Budget, 11th. March 1842.

974. J. Morley, op. cit., p. 240
   R. Cobden to F. Cobden, 12 th. March 1842 - 'Peel delivered
his statement in a clear and clever way, never faltering nor
missing a word in nearly a four hours' speech. This has gone far
to convince our noodles on the Whig side that there is a great
deal of good in his budget.... But I fully expect that it will do
much to render Peel vastly unpopular with the upper portion of
the middle class, who will see no compensation in the tariff for a
tax upon their incomes and profits. If this be the result of the
measure, it will do good to the Corn Law cause by bringing the
discontented to our ranks.'

975. SRP, vol. IV, pp. 57-60
976. Hansard's Parliamentary Debates, Third Series, vol.
   LXIII, pp. 13-91
977. Mark Hovell, The Chartist Movement (Manchester
   University Press, 1943), pp. 257-258
978. Neil Stewart, The Fight for the Charter (Chapman &
   Hall, 1937), pp. 174-175
979. D. Read, Peel and the Victorians, p. 117
   Peel and the Chartist National Petition, 3rd. May 1842.

980. CSP, vol. II, p. 243
981. Sir Edwin Hodder, Life and Work of Shaftesbury (Cassell,
   1887), pp.188-189
982. J. Wesley Bready, Shaftesbury and Industrial Progress
   (Allen & Unwin, 1926), p. 78
983. Florence M.G. Higham, Lord Shaftesbury (SCM Press,
   1945), pp. 37-44
984. AR, pp. 299-301

985. NG2, pp. 334-336
   The Mines Act of 1842

986. BL, Aberdeen Papers, Add. MSS. 43062, f. 48
987. CSP, vol. III, p. 388
988. NG2, p. 500
   16th. May 1842, Peel on the Maine - New Brunswick boundary
dispute with the U.S.A. - 'Seeing that the boundary question
invades no principle, I would go as far as we could safely go, in
the present state of the Canadas, in accommodating matters in so
far as that Question is concerned.'

989. CCD, vol. II, pp. 382-383
   Peel to Croker, 27th.July 1842 - 'Look at the state of society
in this country; the congregation of manufacturing masses; the
amount of our debt; the rapid increase of poor rates within the
last four years,... and then judge whether we can in safety
retrograde in manufactures.... If you had to constitute new
societies, you might on moral and social grounds prefer corn
fields to cotton factories, an agricultural to a manufacturing
population. But our lot is cast; we cannot change it, and we
cannot recede.'

990. Henry Ashworth, Recollections of Richard Cobden, M.P.
   and the Anti-Corn Law League (1877), p. 93.
   4th. August 1842 - 'Mr. John Brooks (representing the Anti-
Corn Law League) of Manchester described the state of distress
existing in that town and spoke of the feverish discontent as
evidently leading to political troubles. Sir James (Graham)
interrupted him, exclaiming, "Why you are a Chartist!"'

991. Royal Archives, A 28 - Peel to Prince Albert, 20th.
   January 1843; A 13 - Peel to Queen Victoria, 25th.,
   26th., 31st. January 1843
992. LV, vol. I, pp. 455-458
993. CSP, vol. II, pp. 552-555
994. GM, 26th., 29th. January 1843
995. Annual Register, 1843
996. R.M. Bousfield & R. Merrett, Report of the Trial of
   Daniel MacNaghton (1843)
997. NG2, pp. 364-366
   Murder of Edward Drummond, 20th.January 1843.

998. SRP, vol. IV, p.149
999. J. Morley, Richard Cobden, pp. 258-261
1000. Wendy Hinde, Richard Cobden, A Victorian Outsider (Yale
   University Press, New Haven, 1987), pp. 118-122
1001. CSP, vol. II, pp. 557-558
1002. NG2,pp. 366-369
   Peel's quarrel with Cobden, 1843

1003. CSP, vol. II, pp. 468-474
1004. AR, pp. 241-248
1005. NG2, pp. 378ff
   Peel and the Disruption of the Church of Scotland,1843.

1006. J. Brooke & Mary Sorensen (eds.), <u>The Prime Minister's</u>
<u>Papers: W.E. Gladstone II: Autobiographical Memoranda,</u>
<u>1832-1845</u> (OUP, 1972), p. 194
    Gladstone on Peel's ideas of the value of parliamentary
speeches, 1843 - 'Fremantle judges a speech according to its
influence on those whom he has to <u>whip</u>; Peel's is a more complex
view made up of the direct influence upon his voting supporters,
the good aspect in argument towards the Opposition for debate and
the general relation to public opinion and the character of the
Administration out of doors.'

1007. Royal Archives, Windsor, F21/1 (October 1843)
1008. NG2, p. 389
1009. Roger Fulford, <u>The Prince Consort</u>, pp. 78-79
1010. Stanley Weintraub, <u>Victoria, Biography of a Queen</u>,
    pp.182-183
    Peel's part in the purchase of Osborne House on the Isle of
Wight by Victoria and Albert, 1843-1844.

1011. David Kynaston, <u>The City of London, 1815-1890,</u>
    (2 vols., Chatto & Windus, 1994), vol. I, p. 124
    Joshua Bates of Baring Brothers and Company (Bankers), 1843 -
'All the doings of Sir Robert Peel in the Tariff, etc. by which he
inclines towards the free trade system have been wrong, not only
wrong in the abstract, but wrong in reference to the condition of
the country, its debt, poor laws, etc.'

1012. AR, pp. 275-277
1013. NG2, pp. 408-411
    Trial of Daniel O'Connell.

1014. AR, p. 305
1015. NG2, pp.408-411
1016. D.R. Fisher, 'Peel and the Conservative Party: The
    Sugar Crisis of 1844 Reconsidered,' <u>Historical Journal</u>,
    vol. XVIII (1975), pp. 172-185

1017. <u>Lieven-Palmerston Correspondence</u>, p. 259
    Lady Palmerston to Princess Lieven, 1st. March 1844 - 'You
are right in saying that Peel's position is better than before
the opening of Parliament. His promise to make no other changes
in the Corn Bill had had the effect of rallying those whom he had
previously annoyed, and the prosecution of O'Connell, although
badly arranged and badly carried through and too late, has
nevertheless had a good effect on the country.'

1018. <u>The Times</u>, 7th. May 1844
1019. <u>Northern Star</u>, 11th. May 1844
    A condensation of Peel's speech of 6th. May 1844 on his
banking reforms (SRP, vol. IV, pp. 347ff) - 'First, he would
enquire what was a pound? Surely the word "pound" meant something
more than an abstraction; in his opinion it meant a certain
weight of precious metal of a certain fineness; and the
engagement of a maker of a promissory note to pay on demand a
definite amount of that metal and fineness. A real measure of
value in that just sense had existed till the year 1797.'

1020. Bl, Add. Mss. 43063, f. 324
1021. NG2, p. 511
    Peel to Aberdeen, 21st. August 1844 - 'I do most earnestly
advise that we should without delay consider the state of our
naval preparation as compared with that of France. Matters are in
that state that the interval of twenty-four hours - some act of
violence for which the French ministry is not strong enough to
makereparation or disavowal - may not only dissipate the shadow
of the Entente Cordiale, but change our relations from peace to
war. Let us be prepared for war. Some may think the preparations
for it will diminish the chance of peace, that the fact of our
strengthening ourselves may give alarm or umbrage to the French.
My belief is, from all I have seen of the French people and their
government, that they are much more likely to presume upon our
weakness than to take offence at our strength.'

1022. BL, Add. MSS. 4054, f. 124
1023. NG2, p. 504
    Peel to Aberdeen, September 1844 - 'I should not be afraid of a
good deal of preliminary bluster on the part of the Americans.
The best answer would be to direct the Collingwood to make a
friendly visit when she has leisure to the mouth of the
Columbia.

1024. BL, Add. MSS. 4054, f. 218
1025. NG2, p. 513
    Peel to Aberdeen, 20th. December 1844 - 'If the King of the
French is, as I dare say he is, mediating an alliance between the
Duc de Monpensier and the sister of the Queen of Spain, the
proceeding is underhand and dishnest. It is not an actual breach
of honourable engagement to this country, but considering the
state of health of the Queen of Spain, the effect will not
probably be very different from an alliance with the Queen
herself - and there is but little prospect of a bone fide Entente
Cordiale between England and France, if we are constantly on the
look out for being cleverly overreached. Entente Cordiale
implies at least frank and honest declarations of intentions.

1026. AR, p. 310
    On 13th. March 1845, while Cobden spoke in the House of
Commons against the Corn Laws, Peel finally said to Sidney
Herbert, sitting next to him, 'You must answer this, for I
cannot.'

1027. CCD, vol II, p. 31
    Graham to Croker, 22nd. March 1845 - 'If we have lost the
confidence and good will of the country party, our official days
are numbered; and the time will come when this party will
bitterly deplore of Sir Robert Peel, and when in vain they will
wish they had not overthrown a Government which its enemies could
not vanquish, but which its supporters abandoned and
undermined.'

1028. Lord Rosebery, Sir Robert Peel, p. 19
    Prince Albert to Stockmar, July 1845 - 'In politics we are
draw-ing near to the close of one of the most remarkable sittings
of Parliament. Peel has carried through everything with immense
majorities, but it is certain that he has no longer any stable
parliamentary support. His party is quite broken up and the

opposition has as many opinions and principles as heads.

1029. D. Read, Peel and the Victorians, pp. 138-145
1030. AR, pp. 279, 280, 282, 301
1031. NG2, pp. 129, 140, 149-150, 607
1032. D.C. Lathbury (ed.), Letters on Church and Religion of
      William Ewart Gladstone (John Murray, 2 vols., 1910),
      vol. I, pp. 51, 52, 62ff; vol. II, p. 4

1033. Philip Magnus, Gladstone (John Murray, 1963), pp. 67-70
1034. Robert Blake, Disraeli (Methuen, 1969), pp. 188-189
1035. G.O. Trevelyan, Life and Letters of Lord Macaulay
      (Longmans, Green, 1890), p. 452
      The Maynooth Grant, 1845.

1036. The Times, 6th.November 1845
    'The present corn laws are doomed. It is for the Premier to
decide whether he will sign the warrant for their execution....
The most prudent of Premiers may hesitate before he condemns what
he has sanctioned and sanctions what he strenuously denounced.
If this be so, there is only one course for him to take - to
abstain from taking an open part in this important question - and
to leave to others the merit of settling the question and to
RESIGN.'

1037. Lord John Russell, Letter to the Electors of the City
      of London ('Edinburgh Letter'), 22nd. November 1845
    'The Government seems to be waiting for some excuse to give up
the present Corn Law. Let the people by petition, by address, by
remonstrance, afford them the excuse they seek.'

1038. LV, vol. II, p. 47
    Victoria to Peel, 28th. November 1845 - 'The Queen thinks the
time is come when a removal of restrictions upon the importation
of food cannot be successfully resisted.Should this be Sir
Robert's own opinion, the Queen very much hopes that none of his
colleagues will prevent him doing what it is right to do.'

1039. The Times, 4th. December 1845
    'The decision of the Cabinet is no longer a secret. Parliament
is to be summoned for the first week in January, and the Royal
Speech will recommend an immediate consideration of the Corn
Laws, preparatory to their total repeal. By the end of January at
the latest, the produce of all countries will enter the British
market on an absolute equality with our own.'

1040. Sunday Times, 7th. December 1845
    'It appears to be at length pretty certain that the end of the
Corn-laws is rapidly approaching, and the question now is, who
deals them the fatal blow? There need not, however, be much doubt
about the matter.... The Tory ministers have done something, the
Liberal ex-ministers have done more; but the great agent in the
business has been the Anti-Corn Law League. No one in his senses
can deny this. Without the kind assistance of the League, the
Corn Laws would probably have perished some day or another,
because it is not in the nature of injustice to be everlasting;
but we much fear they would have outlived the present generation
and sent many thousands and tens of thousands prematurely to
their graves.

1041. <u>Morning Post</u>, 12th. December 1845
  'His (Peel's) whole career since 1842 has been one of insanity or treachery. We have done all in our power to expose him. He has not - since 1842 - deceived <u>us</u>. We regard him as the most loathsome of public men. His abilities - which are questionable - only add to his odiousness. He prostitutes to the meanest purpose the talents which God has given him. We hope that there can now be no doubt of his joining the Whigs. That the Tories should ever again have anything to do with him, we cannot suppose.'

1042. CSP, vol. III, pp. 254-255
1043. NG2, p. 560
  Peel to Sir Thomas Fremantle, 19th. December 1845 - 'I heartily rejoice at being relieved from the thankless and dangerous post of having the responsibility of conducting public affairs and being expected to conform, not to my own sense of public necessities, but to certain party doctrines, to be blindly followed whatever new circumstances may arise.... Whatever country squires may think, it is not safe to guarantee the continuation of the present Corn Laws.

1044. D. Read, <u>Peel and the Victorians</u>, p. 193
1045. LV, vol. II, p. 66
  Prince Albert's Memorandum of 25th. December 1845 - 'Sir Robert has <u>an immense scheme in view</u>; he thinks he shall be able to remove the contest entirely from the dangerous ground upon which it had got - that of a war between the manufacturers, the hungry and the poor against the landed proprietors, the aristocracy, which can only end in the ruin of the latter; he will not only bring a measure upon the Corn Law, but a much more comprehensive one. He will deal with the whole commercial system of the country. He will adopt the principle of the League, <u>that of removing all protection and abolishing all monopoly</u>, but not in favour of one class and as a triumph over another, but to the benefit of the nation, farmers as well as manufacturers.

1046. LV, vol. II, p. 63
  Peel to Victoria, 31st. December 1845 - 'Sir Robert Peel has written very strongly ... to the Duke (of Buccleugh), stating that the present position is not one of Corn Law, but whether your Majesty's former servants or Lord Grey and Mr. Cobden shall constitute your Majesty's Government. Sir Robert Peel defied the wit of man to suggest now another alternative to your Majesty.'

1047. SRP, vol. IV, pp. 567-717
  Peel's Corn Law speeches, 1846

1048. <u>Maidstone Gazette</u>, 6th. January 1846
  'Sir Robert Peel knows well that the Corn Law question must and will be settled; not at the instance of the persons maintaining these laws or getting them abolished; but by the means of moderate men, who may be said to be the depositories of that strong common sense for which our nation is celebrated; who seldom take an active part in politics, but who inevitably throw their weight into the scale of opposition to every proved and tangible grievance. Such the present Corn Laws are now admitted to be.

1049. BL, Add. MSS. 40484, f.263
   Peel to Arbuthnot, 7th. January 1846 - 'I can demonstrate that
everything that has been done has been for the benefit not merely
of the Community at large, but of the Agricultural interest. Wool
bears a higher price than it did before the reduction of the duty
on foreign Wool. So does Meat. So do Bullocks and Cows and Sheep
about which there was so much absurd panic. The agricultural
labourers have been better off this Winter and the last than they
were before.

1050. GM, 30th. January 1846
1051. David Cecil, Lord M, . p. 267
   Lord Melbourne's opinion of Peel's change of attitude towards
the Corn Laws.

1052. MC, vol. II, p. 265
1053. NG2, pp.584-585
   Peel to the Duke of Richmond, President of the Central
Agricultural Protection Society, 14th.January 1846 - 'I see that
the Protection Society has repealed its rule which prevents
interference in elections and proposes to fight the Anti-Corn
Law League with their own weapons; that is, by multiplying the
lower class of country voters. All this will tell ultimately in
favour of democracy when the excitement of the moment shall have
subsided. The 40/- freeholders in Ireland were an instrument
used against the landlords.'

1054. D. Read, op. cit., pp. 215-216
1055. Hansard, vol. LXXXIV, pp. 248-249
1056. Harriet Martineau, Autobiography (2 vols., 1877),
      vol. II, pp. 259-264
1057. J. Morley, Richard Cobden, pp. 350-354
1058. W. Hinde, Richard Cobden, pp. 160-161, 163-166
1059. CSP, vol. III, pp. 328-332
1060. NG2, pp. 576-577
   Peel's reconciliation with Cobden, 1846.

1061. Daily News, 21st. January 1846
   'The principles advocated by THE DAILY NEWS will be
Principles of Progress and Improvement; of Education, Civil and
Religious Liberty and Equal Legislation; Principles, such as its
conductors believe the advancing spirit of the time requires:
the condition of the country demands: and Justice, Reason and
Experience legitimately sanction. Very much is to be done and
must be done towards the bodily comfort, mental elevation and
general contentment of the English people. But, the social
improvement is so inseparable from the well-doing of Arts and
Commerce, the growth of public works, the free investment of
capital in all those numerous helps to civilisation and
improvement to which the ingenuity of the ages gives birth, that
we hold it to be impossible rationally to consider the true
interest of the people as a class-question or to separate them
from the interests of the merchant and manufacturer.

1062. CSP, vol. IV, pp. 567-581
1063. GM, 23rd. January 1846
1064. R. Edgcumbe, op. cit., p. 217
1065. NG2, pp. 567-568
   Peel's speech at Parliament's opening, 2nd.January 1846.

1066. <u>Northern Star</u>, 31st. January 1846
   'Now, had free trade proposed in the Whig style - had it been
granted as boon to the increasing power of the League and as sop
to the monied interests, unaccompanied by those wise, salutary
and statesmanlike adjustments proposed by Sir Robert Peel, not
all the power at the disposal of government could have averted
the horrors of revolution.'

1067.<u>Daily News</u>, 17th. February 1846
   'It is seldom that statesmen or orators, on the Tory side of
politics, can draw from that great source of inspiration - the
feeling that they struggle for popular rights and minister to the
necessities of the people. Sir Robert Peel seemed, however, to
have felt the charm and power of that inspiration and felt it the
more from its being new.'

1068. CSP, vol. III, p.331
   Harriet Martineau to Peel, 22nd. February 1846 - 'You are a
great doer of the impossible, in the government of yourself as
well as in the government of the country. In the administration
of public affairs, as surely as a great act or measure is declared
impracticable, you forthwith achieve it.'

1069. J. Morley, <u>op. cit.</u>, p.366
   Cobden to George Combe, 7th. March 1846 - 'Among all the
converts and conformers, I class Sir Robert Peel as one of the
most sincere and earnest. I have no doubt he is acting from strong
conviction. His mind has a natural leading towards politico-
economical truths. The man, who could make it his hobby so early
to work out the dry problems of the currency question and arrive
at such sound conclusions, could not fail to be equally able and
willing to put into practice the other theories of Adam
Smith.'

1070. <u>Daily News</u>, 14th. March 1846
   'Appropriate - Sir R. Peel returned from Brighton by the mail
train on Sunday. The Duke of Richmond was a passenger by the same
train, but these two distinguished passengers did not travel in
the same carriage. As if to illustrate the positions they
respectively occupy in the country, Sir Robert placed himself in
the leading <u>coupé</u>, and the Duke got into the <u>coupé</u> which is at the
tail of the train.'

1071. <u>Croker Papers</u> (ed. Pool), pp. 202-203
   Croker to Sir Henry Hardinge, 24th. April 1846 - 'The fatal
consequences are that Peel, by betraying the precise and
specific principle upom which he was brought into office, had
ruined the character of public men and dissolved, by dividing,
the great landed interest - the only solid foundation on which
any government can be formed in this country....'

1072. <u>The Speech of Mr. Disraeli Delivered in the House of
        Commons on Friday, May 15, 1846</u> (1846)
   'When the minister (Peel) last met the House and his party, he
acted as if we had deserted him, instead of his having left us
(<u>great cheering</u>). Who can forget those tones? Who can forget that
indignant glance? ... which seems to say, "I, a protectionist
minister, mean to govern England by the aid of the Anti-Corn Law
League (<u>cheers</u>). And, as for the country gentlemen, why I snap my

fingers in their face." (<u>continued cheers</u>).'

1073. GM, 21st. May 1846
    'Last week the debate in the House of Commons came to a close,
wound by a speech of Disraeli's, very clever, in which he hacked
and mangled Peel with the most unsparing severity and positively
tortured his victim. It was a miserable and degrading spectacle.
The whole mass of the Protectionists cheered him with vociferous
delight, making the roof ring again, and when Peel spoke, they
screamed and hooted at him in the most brutal manner. When he
vindicated himself and talked of honour and conscience, they
assailed him with shouts of derision and gestures of
contempt.... They hunt him like a fox, and they are eager to run
him down and kill him in the open, and they are full of exultation
at thinking that they have nearly accomplished this object.'

1074. PRO, Broadlands Papers, SHA/PD/4
    Lord Ashley's Diary, 22nd. May 1846 - 'No one believes that
Peel could have foreseen the tenth part of the sensation that has
been caused by his political conduct. I cannot conceive that the
notion crossed his imagination. He calculated, and despised an
expression of feeling; a small band of dissidents, a large band
of turncoats, a week's debate, a large majority, triumph and
commendations, and the total oblivion of the whole matter.'

1075. <u>Hansard</u>, Third Series, vol. LXXXVII, pp. 177-184
1076. Goldwin Smith, <u>Reminiscences</u> (Macmillan, 1910),
        p. 176
1077. J. Martineau, <u>Life of the Fifth Duke of Newcastle</u>
        (1881), p. 80
1078. BL, Add. MSS. 4052, ff. 118, 120; 4055, ff. 361-370
1079. SRP, vol. IV, p.709
1080. GM, 27th. June 1846
1081. LV, vol. II, p. 79 (Royal Archives, C24/951)
1082. NG2, pp. 595-598
    The Canning Incident, 8th. - 19th. June 1846

1083. <u>Examiner</u>, 20th.June 1846
    'The popularity of what at best is next to a death-bed
repentance is only the express sign of the demoralization.... A
portion of the public is becoming of opinion that honesty is not
the best policy.... Both the hatred and the popularity that folow
Sir Robert are in bad extremes and of evil tendencies. He makes
the worst enemies and not the most principled friends.'

1084. J. Morley, <u>op. cit.</u>, pp. 390-401
1085. MC, vol. II, p. 309
1086. W.O. Aydelotte, 'The Country Gentlemen and the Repeal
        of the Corn Laws, <u>English Historical Review</u>, vol.
        LXXXII (1974), pp. 58-59
1087. R. Blake, <u>Disraeli</u>, pp. 235-236, 240-241
    The Irish Coercion Bill, 1846.

1088. Benjamin Disraeli, <u>Lord George Bentinck</u>, pp. 184-196
    Disrael's account of Peel's defeat on the Irish Coercion
    Bill, 25th. June 1846.
    'They trooped on: all the men of metal and large-acred
squires, whose spirit he had so often quickened and whose counsel
he had so often solicited in his fine Conservative speeches

in Whitehall Gardens....
The news that the government were not only beaten, but by a majority so large as 73, began to circulate. An incredulous murmur passed it along the treasury bench.
'They say we are beaten by 73!' whispered the most important member of the cabinet in a tone of surprise to Sir Robert Peel.
Sir Robert did not reply or even turn his head. He looked very grave and extended his chin as was his habit when he was annoyed and cared not to speak. He began to comprehend his position and that the emperor was without his army.'

1089. LV, vol. II, pp. 80-82
1090. BL, Add. MSS. 44777, f. 245 (Gladstone Papers)
1091. Royal Archives, C/25/4 (Peel to Victoria)
1092. Comte de Jarnac, Revue des Deux Mondes (July 1874), pp. 284ff
1093. NG2, pp. 602-604
Peel's resignation from the Premiership.

1094. Diaries of Lady Charlotte Guest, p. 181.
26th. June 1846. The Lords having passed the Corn Bill, which received the royal assent to-night, there was a division last night in the Commons on the Irish Coercion Bill in which Peel was left in a minority of 77, and so his ministry, which has been a glorious one, is ended. All Whig as I am, I must bear honourable testimony to his brilliant career and the excellency of the measure he has so triumphantly carried against all the prejudices and violence of the monopolists.'

1095. Morning Post, 27th. June 1846
'Waiving the question of the national effects of his policy, we hold that his cold deceit - his treachery to those who trusted him - is far too palpable to be denied by any honest and observing man; and this offence now committed for the second time, deserves every public reproach and public disgrace that can befall him. His position in history, if he holds any position at all, ought, in our judgment, to be among the infamous.'

1096. Sunday Times, 28th. June 1846
'When the poor in millions of cottages are enjoying the blessings of untaxed bread - when our numerous colonies are found springing into immensely- increasing importance through having the shackles of monopoly removed from their exertions, the name of Sir Robert Peel will be remembered and respected with gratitude and honour.'

1097. Morning Chronicle, 29th. June 1846
'There seems to be a very general disposition among all sections of the Liberal party to abstain from anything like searching and severe criticism of that extraordinary series of moral phenomena comprised within the last ten or twelve years of Sir Robert Peel's life.'

1098. The Times, 30th. June 1846
'How long was it urged as a solemn obligation on all devout Conservatives to abhor the League and anathemize Cobden? Popular movements of all sorts were denounced as injurious to good order.... Now, from the lips of the Premier, we are told that

the name of Richard Cobden is associated with one of the greatest
measures of social reform known to modern times.'

1099. Daily News, 30th. June 1846
'The sacrifice of life and power for a great end; that
sacrifice made, moreover, in the plenitude of life and power and
made with strong foresight and firm will: all these ennoble. They
leave no room for pity, none for contempt. They silence hatred
and redeem many faults.'

1100. Morning Herald, 30th. June 1846
'His (Peel's) offence is not merely an offence against party,
but against morals.

1101. LV, vol. II, p. 87
Victoria to King Leopold, 7th. July 1846 - 'I have had to part
with Sir R. Peel and Lord Aberdeen, who are irreparable losses to
us and the country; they were both so overcome that it quite
upset me, and we have in them two devoted friends. We felt safe
with them.... Then the discretion of Peel, I believe, is
unexampled.'

LAST YEARS (1846-1850)

1102. NG2, pp. 603-604
Peel's resignation speech in the House of Commons, 29th. June
1846 - 'I shall leave a name execrated by every monopolist, but
it may be ... sometimes remembered with expressions of good-will
in the abodes of those whose lot it2
is to labour and earn their daily bread by the sweat of their
brow, when they shall recruit their exhausted strength with
abundant and untaxed food, the sweeter because it is no longer
unleavened with a sense of injustice.'

1103. CSP, vol. III, p.474
Peel to Sir Henry Hardinge, 24th. September 1846 - 'I intend
to keep aloof from party combinations. So far as a man can be
justified in forming such a resolution, I am determined not again
to resume office. I would be nothing but the head of a Government,
the real bona-fide head, and to be that requires more youth, more
ambition, more love of official power and official occupation
than I can pretend to. I will take care not again to burn my
fingers by organizing a party. There is too much truth in the
saying, "The head of a party must be directed by the tail."'

1104. Althea Hayter, A Sultry Month (Longmans, 1965,) p. 147
Peel's generosity to the widow of Robert Haydon, the
historical artist, who committed suicide on 22nd. June 1846.

1105. A.E. Watkin (ed.), Absolam Watkin, Extracts from his
      Journal (Fisher Unwin, 1920)
1106. Magdalen Goffin (ed.), The Diaries of Absolam Watkin,
      A Manchester Man, 1787-1861 (Alan Sutton, 1993)
26th. June 1847, the opening of the Trent Valley Railway Line
by Peel - 'The great attraction was Sir Robert Peel, and his
speech was, of course, the speech of the day, and I was much
pleased. He has a gentle, manly bearing and carried his head
well; his features are good, the mouth being well-formed and the
eye not bright, yet not dull. He seems to smile habitually,

but the line of care and, as I thought, of cunning, are very visible in his countenance. His voice is good, his utterance extremely distinct and his sentences well-formed.'

1107. J.A. Froude, Life of Thomas Carlyle (4 vols., Longmans, Green, 1882-1884), vol. I, p. 433
Carlyle's meeting with Peel in 1848 -'He is towards sixty and, though not broken at all, carries especially in his complexion when you are near him, marks of that age: clear strong blue eyes which kindle on occasions, voice extremely good, low-toned, something of cooing in it, rustic, affectionate, honest, mildly persuasive.... Reserved seemingly by nature, obtrudes nothing of diplomatic reserve. On the contrary, a vein of mild fun in him, real sensibility to the ludicrous, which feature I liked best of all.'

1108. John Morley, Life of Gladstone (Edward Lloyd, 2 vols., 1908), vol. I, p. 276
Gladstone to his father, 2nd. July 1850 - 'I thought Sir R. Peel looked extremely feeble during the debate last week. I mean as compared with what he usually is. I observed that he slept during much of Lord Palmerston's speech, that he spoke with very little physical energy, and the next day, Saturday, in the forenoon I thought he looked very ill at a meeting (of the Commission on the 1851 Exhibition) which, in common with him I had to attend.'

1109. The Times, 3rd.July 1850
'On Friday the House of Commons, which for more than forty years has witnessed, the triumphs and reverses of the great Conservative chief, was filled with an extraordinary assemblage anxious for the result of a great political crisis. Sir Robert addressed them with ability and a spirit which recalled his more youthful efforts and more powerful days. It was the first occasion for four years that elicited any serious or direct opposition to the policy of Her Majesty's present advisers, and ... it must be allowed that the speech was at least an admirable defence of the principles on which Sir Robert and his colleagues had ever proceeded.'
The Don Pacifico Debate, 28th. June 1850.

1110. James Lees-Milne, The Bachelor Duke, William Spencer Cavendish, Sixth Duke of Devonshire, 1790-1858 (John Murray, 1991), p. 190
At a meeting of the Royal Commissioners for the 1851 Exhibition on 29th. June 1850, Joseph Paxton, the Head Gardener of the Duke of Devonshire at Chatsworth in Derbyshire, put forward his scheme for a glass Crystal Palace to contain the Exhibition in Hyde Park, London. Peel's strong support for this probably secured its acceptance at that meeting. Later in the day, he went riding and met with the accident which resulted in his death.

1111. The Times, 3rd. July 1850
'Sir Robert Peel expired in the dining-room of his mansion from which apartment he had not been removed since his arrival at home after the accident which has ended so fatally.
Sir Benjamin Brodie, Mr. Caesar Hawkins, Mr. Hodgson, Dr. Seymour, Mr. Shaw and Dr. Foucart have been in attendance

upon Sir Robert since the accident. The latter gentleman is a
Scotch physician resident in Glasgow, who happened to be passing
when the accident occurred. He was one of the first to raise Sir
Robert from the ground and accompanied him in Mrs. Lucas's
carriage home, where he has since continued in constant
attendance with the full concurrence and sanction of Sir
Benjamin Brodie and Mr. Hawkins.'

1112. G.O. Trevelyan, Life and Letters of Lord Macaulay,
        p. 540.
Extracts from Macaulay's Diary:
   '3rd. July 1850. As we drove into Glasgow, I saw "Death of Sir
Robert Peel" placarded at a newsman's. I was extremely shocked.
Thank God I had shaken hands cordially with the poor fellow after
all our blows given and received.
   4th. July 1850. Poor Peel's death in The Times. I have been
more affected by it than I could have believed. It was in the
dining-room that he died. I dined with him there for the first and
last time about a month ago (on 1st. June). If he is to be buried
publicly, I will certainly follow his coffin. Once I little
thought that I could have cried for his death.'

1113. Diaries of Lady Charlotte Guest, p. 245
   '3rd. July 1850. I cannot describe the gloom which this news
(of Peel's death) shed. He was a great man, the greatest man in
Europe, and though I differed from him in politics, I regret him
more than I could have done any other public man. It is a curious
coincidence that he should have spoken the night before his
accident against ministers, with whom for so many years he has
now appeared to coincide.'

1114. The Times, 4th. July 1850
1115. Lancet, 6th. July 1850
1116. BL, Peel Papers, Add. MSS. 40609, ff. 369-377
1117. T. Holmes, Sir Benjamin Brodie (Macmillan, 1898),
        App. M
1118. NG2, pp. 701-702
    Peel's fatal injuries.

1119. Chamber's Papers for the People, 4th. July 1850
   'He (Peel) fell from official power into the arms of the
people, whose enthusiastic plaudits accompanied him. on the
evening of his resignation from office, to his residence in
Whitehall Gardens.... They felt instinctively that he must be
ours and single-minded, as he was intellectually vigorous and
great; for what was he, raised aloft upon the bucklers of a
powerful and wealthy party, to gain by stooping from that
dazzling height, to raise up the humble and lowly from the mire
into which ignorant and partial legislation had so long trampled
them.'

1120. Lord Rosebery, Sir Robert Peel (1899), p. 95
   'On the night of his (Peel's) resignation, a silent multitude
awaited him as he left the House of Commons and, with bared heads,
escorted him home. As he lay dying, a sadder crowd surrounded
that home day and night, waiting breathlessly for tidings of the
father of their country.'

1121. Trudy Bliss (ed.), <u>Letters of Jane Welsh Carlyle</u>
      (Arrow Books, 1959), p. 208)
      Mrs. Carlyle to Helen Welsh, 4th. July 1850 - 'This death
(Peel's) has produced a greater dismay than any public event of
my time - not only among his own set, but crowds of working people
pressed round his house all the time of his illness demanding
news which a constable, lifted above their heads, tried to make
them hear in vain - and written bulletins were finally hoisted up
to be read by the crowd from hour to hour.'

1122. <u>Morning Chronicle</u>, 5th. July 1850
      An anonymous article (written by Gladstone) - 'Without
contrasts he (Peel) could never have made the sacrifices -
without the sacrifices he could never have made the efforts and
endured the agonies of the critical periods of his life -
without the efforts and the agonies he could never have realized
the growth - his understanding never could have been educated
into the strength and elasticity, the largeness and the
fineness, for which it was alike marvellous.'

1123. LV, vol. II, pp. 254-255
      The King of the Belgians to Queen Victoria, 5th. July 1850 -
It gives me the greatest pain to learn of the death of our true
and kind friend, Sir Robert Peel, That he should have met with
his end - so valuable to the whole earth - from an accident so
easily to be avoided with some care, is the more to be lamented.
You and Albert lose in him a friend whose moderation, correct
judgment, great knowledge of everything connected with the
country, can never be found again. Europe had in him a benevolent
and truly wise statesman....'

1124. <u>Manchester Guardian</u>, 6th. July 1850
      'Round the details of a tariff he (Peel) threw a charm from
which none could escape; and after listening to him for hours on
cotton wool, copper ore, the duties on glass, exports and
imports, bank issues, national income and expenditure, you
wondered by what magic he contrived to fascinate you with topics
so heavy in the hands of other men.'

1125. LV, vol. II, p. 256
      Queen Victoria to the King of the Belgians, 9th. July 1850 -
'The sorrow and grief at his (Peel's) death are very touching,
and the country mourns over him as over a father. Everyone seems
to have lost a personal friend.... My poor dear Albert, who had
been so fresh and well when we came back, looks pale and fagged
again. He has felt and feels Sir Robert's loss <u>dreadfully</u>. He
feels he has lost a second father.'

1126. <u>The Times</u>, 10th.July 1850
1127. <u>Morning Chronicle</u>, 10th. July 1850
1128. <u>Illustrated London News</u>, 13th. July 1850
      Peel's funeral.

1129. 'One Who Thinks for Himself,' <u>Peel A Mystery, The Man
      and His Motives Made Plain</u> (August 1850)
1130. D. Read, <u>Peel and the Victorians</u>, p. 1
      'Even at the expense of being thought guilty of an Irishism,
we must own that we would have liked Peel to have lived a month
after his death, in order that he might have enjoyed to the

full his posthumous fame. How he would have revelled in every
daily and weekly newspaper, how blandly he would have pondered
over every review, how charmed he would have been with the bright
light thrown on his darkest actions, and how surely would the
close of the month have found him feeling in his pockets to
subscribe to every one of his intended statues.'

1131. Surrey Record Office, Goulburn Papers
     MS. Catalogue of Books, etc. at no. 4 Whitehall Gardens.

1132. T. Martin, Life of the Prince Consort (Smith Elder, 5
     vols., 1876), vol. II, p. 290
     Albert to Duchess of Kent, 4th. July 1850 - 'Death has
snatched from us Peel, the best of men, our truest friend, the
strongest bulwark of the throne, the greatest statesman of his
time.'

1133. J. Timbs, A Century of Anecdotes from 1760 to 1860
     (Frederick Warne, n.d.), p. 218
1134. Tresham Lever, Life and Times of Peel, p. 302
     Wellington in the House of Lords, 4th. July 1850 - 'In all the
course of my acquaintance with Sir Robert Peel, I never knew a man
in whose truth and justice I had a more lively confidence or in
whom I saw a more invariable desire to promote the public
service.'

1135. J. Martineau, Life of the Fifth Duke of Newcastle (1908),
     p. 99
     Lord Lincoln (Fifth Duke of Newcastle from 1851) - 'The death
of Sir Robert Peel seems yet to me like a horrid dream, a thing
that cannot be... I have ever found in him so delicate a sympathy
and so sagacious advice,that the termination of my married life
and the simultaneous death of a friend and counsellor seem to
leave me in a void which yet appears bewildering.'

1136. H.M. & M. Swartz, Disraeli's Reminiscences
     (Methuen,1975), p. 23
1137. R. Shannon, Gladstone, vol. I,p.224
     'A day or two after Peel's death, Gladstone was at the Carlton
(Club) and said, "Peel died at peace with all mankind; even with
Disraeli. The last thing he did was to cheer Disraeli. It was not
a very loud cheer, but it was a cheer; it was distinct, I sat next
to him."'

1138. Random Recollections of the House of Commons (1837),
     pp. 108-120
1139. Sir Robert Peel and his Era (1844), pp. 254-258
1140. H. Martin, Personal Sketch of Sir Robert Peel (1850)
1141. Sir Robert Peel, Statesman and Orator (1846)
1142. Lord Dalling, Sir Robert Peel (1874), pp. 84-85
     Contemporary descriptions of Peel.

JUDGEMENTS UPON PEEL

1143. Benjamin Disraeli, Lord George Bentinck, p. 32
1144. H.W.C. Davis, The Age of Grey and Peel, p. 300
     Disraeli's opinion - 'When Sir Robert Peel was of opinion that
the Corn Laws must be repealed, he was resolved to be the
repealer.'

1145. GM, 15th. July 1850
    'The misfortune of Peel all along was that there was no real
community of sentiment between him and his party.... They
considered Peel to be not only the minister but the creature of
the Conservative Party, bound above all things to support and
protect their especial interests according to their own views
and opinions. He considered himself the Minister of the
Nation....

1146. Kellow Chesney, The Victorian Underworld, Maurice
        Temple Smith, 1970), pp. 214, 228
    Peel figured prominently on the lists circulated among
beggars giving the names of people likely to respond to appeals
for alms.

1147. Royal Archives, Queen Victoria's Journal
    '12th. November 1851 - 'It was poor Sir Robert's misfortune to
have been kept down to old Tory principles, for which his mind
was far too enlightened.'

1148. Anthony Trollope, The Three Clerks (1858), chap. VI
    'He (Peel) has taught us a great lesson, that a man who has
before him a mighty object may dispense with those old-fashioned
rules of truth to his neighbours and honesty to his own
principles, which should guide us in ordinary life. At what point
ordinary life ends, at what crisis objects may be great enough to
justify the use of a dispensing power,that he has not taught
us.'

1149. Benjamin Disraeli, Lord George Bentinck, p. 303
    'For a very clever man, he was deficient in the knowledge of
human nature. The prosperous routine of his youth was not
favourable to the development of this faculty. It was never his
lot to struggle; although forty years in Parliament, it is
remarkable that Sir Robert Peel never represented a popular
constituency or stood a contested election.'

1150. Asa Briggs, Victorian Things (Penguin Books, 1988),
        p. 149
    Inscription on a Staffordshire pottery jug commemorating
Peel - Farewell great statesman. Long will thy honest worth be
missed in the Councils of Nations. And when the time of England's
difficulty comes, then will the people truly feel the Patriot
they have lost in Robert Peel.'

1151. D. Read, Peel and the Victorians, p. 304
    Inscription on a mourning medal for Peel now in the British
Museum - 'His death was deeply deplored by all men of all shades
of political opinion, as the loss of a great practical statesman,
earnestly devoted to the welfare of his country and a generous
friend to literature and art.'
And even very accessible to popular impressions in regard to
national dignity and honour, he (Peel) formed no desire of
aggrandisement for England, felt no selfish jealousy of foreign
nations and had no mania for domination abroad.... He respects
the rights and dignity of other states, small as well as

great, weak as well as strong - and regarded the employment of menace or force solely as a last extremity, legitimate only when it was absolutely necessary....'

1153. The Times, 30th. August 1855
'Peel's symbolical is quite separate from his personal character. While the latter is liable to infinite controversy and misconception, the former is clear from all doubt and difficulty. The last action of his political life has completely eclipsed all the others, and the statues that rise to his memory stand simply and solely as the effigy of the man who broke the fetters of Protection.'

1154. J. Morley, Richard Cobden, p.237
'My (Cobden's) own conviction is that Peel was always a Free Trader in theory; in fact, on all politic-economic questions, he was always as sound in the abstract as Adam Smith or Bentham. For he was peculiarly a politico-economical, and not a Protectionist, intellect. But he never believed that absolute Free Trade came within the category of practical House of Commons questions. It was a question of numbers with him; and as he was yoked with a majority of inferior animals, he was obliged to go their pace and not his own.'

1155. A.C. Benson, Edward White Benson, Archbishop of
        Canterbury (Macmillan,1901),p.50
Gladstone speaking to Benson,29th. August 1895 - 'He said that Sir R. Peel and Prince Albert had the conscience burdened with public duty "more than any two people he had ever known. A most noble sense of duty."'

1156. John Russell, Earl Russell, Recollections and
        Suggestions (1875), p.267
'While I believe that Sir Robert Peel erred from over-caution, I see no reason to doubt that his great capacity was at all times employed for what he believed to be the welfare of his county.'

1157. T.E. Kebbel, History of Toryism (1886), Allen, pp. 336
        342
'His (Peel's) very name seems a synonym for all that is safe, judicious, business-like, sound and practical. In spite of the great schisms of 1829 and 1846, we cannot help looking back upon him as a man whom any party would have been wise to follow. We cannot help it. Nor can I doubt that if he had been spared, his old followers would again have fallen under the spell and again have mustered under his banner.'

1158. Sir Algernon West, Recollections, 1832-1886 (Nelson,
        1899), p. 50
'Peel was by nature cold and reserved, but he was a Parliamentary tactician and master of the House of Commons, endowed with high principles but little imagination. Joseph Hume was an excellent and persevering economist, who was always worrying him on this question, and, coming one evening into the library of the House of Commons, he said, "I shall make a speaker of that fellow Peel yet."'

1159. Reminiscences of Lady Dorothy Nevill (Nelson, 1906),
      p. 342.
      'A first-rate orator and man of exception mental power, Sir
Robert's disposition was unfortunately lacking in stability, a
defect which was especially apparent throughout his career as a
politician. Towards the end of his life he went but little into
society, but, notwithstanding this, I saw him pretty frequently,
as from time to time he used to make a point of coming to pay me a
visit, in order, as he said, to keep up a friendship of very
ancient date.'

1160. G.W.E. Russell, Collections and Recollections (Nelson,
      1903), p. 121
      'As a speaker on public platforms, in the heyday of the ten-
pound householder and the middle-class franchise, he (Peel) was
particularly in his element. He had beyond most men the art of
"making a platitude endurable by making it pompous." He excelled
in demonstrating the material advantages of a moderate and
cautious conservatism, and he could draw at will and with effect
upon a prodigous fund of constitutional commonplaces.'

1161. G.W.E. Russell, Collections and Recollections, Second
      Series (Nelson,190), p. 114
      'His (Peel's) shyness,stiffness and social awkwardness made
him an uncomfortable courtier. "I have no small talk,' said the
Duke of Wellington, "and Peel has no manners." But Peel very
early succeeded in winning the complete confidence of Prince
Albert, and a statesman whom the Prince trusted coould be sure of
his ground with the Queen.'

1162. H.A.L. Fisher, A History of Europe (Edward Arnold, one vol.
      ed., 1936), pp.900-901
      'If England during the latter part of the nineteenth century
became a cheap place to live in, if her trade was worl-wide, and
the whole world was her granary, if a deficit had been turned into
a surplus by the reduction of import duties, if her banking and
currency had been placed on a firm foundation, and her legal
system relieved from many of the worst defects which had been
pointed out by Jeremy Bentham, ... the result is not a little
owing to "the extraordinary abilities and ordinary opinions" of
Sir Robert Peel.'

1163. H.J. Laski, 'Robert Peel, 'H.J. Massingham & Hugh
      Massingham (eds.), The Great Victorians (Pelican ed.,
      1937), p. 415
      'No student of his (Peel's) career will be tempted to forget
the unwearying passion for the public good he displayed in the
last half of his political life, especially in its fourfinal
years; nor is he likly to withold the meed of profound admiration
for the immense abilities he brought to his self-imposed
task.'

1164. G.M. Young, 'Victorian Centenary,' Victorian Essays
(OUP, 1962), p.14
      The suspicions with which old Tories and strong Tories
regarded Peel were justiified. He was not really at hom in the
party, because he would never have been at home in any party. But
he played on the House of Commons like an old fiddle. He was not a
man of wide outlook or deep and far-sighted reflection; so

far his Whig and Radical assailants were right. But he could
make an administration work with the power and precision of a
fine engine.'

THE PEELITES (1846-1859)

1165. CSP, vol. III, pp. 559-560
    Lord Lincoln on Peel - 'He is my leader still, though
invisible. I never take a step in public life without reflecting
how he would have thought of it.'

1166. John Morley, Life of Gladstone, vol I, p. 260
    Gladstone to his father, June 1879 - 'We (the Peelites) have
no party, no organisation, no whipper-in; and under these
circumstances we cannot exercise any considerable degree of
permanent influence as a body.'

1167. Croker Papers (ed. Pool), p.226
    Lord Stanley to Croker, 18th. August 1850 - 'The session which
has just passed was to my mind most unsatisfatory. The apparent
success of the Free Trade policy, as exhibited by the state of the
revenue and the amount of our foreign trade, furnishes a
plausible argument in its favour and blinds the eyes of the
country to the real danger we are incurring. Meanwhile, the most
dangerous men are at this moment the scattered remnants of the
Peelites. I have in this session done everything in my power to
conciliate them; with Aberdeen personally I am on the most
friendly terms; but while they are themselves powerless for
good, they have never failed to give the Government a helping
hand, when, but for them, we could have neutralised or mitigated
much of their measures.'

1168. J.B. Conacher, 'Peel and the Peelites, 1846-1850,'
    English Historical Review,vol. LXXIII (1958), p. 73
    'Henry Goulburn - 'What are we (the Peelites) to do, who
cannot approve of the acts of the Government on the one hand nor
of the acts and opinions of Lord G. Bentinck or D'Israeli on the
other?'

1169. GM,24th. December 1852
    'In the present Cabinet are five or six first-rate men of
equal or nearly equal pretensions, none of them likely to
acknowledge the superiority or defer to the opinions of any
other, and every one of these five or six considering himself
able and more important than their Premier. They are all at
present on very good terms and perfectly satisfied with each
other; but this satisfaction does not extend beyond the Cabinet
itself; murmurings and grumblings are already very loud. The
Whigs have never looked with benignity on this coalition, and
they are now furious at the unequal and, as they think, unfair
distribution of places that every Peelite should be provided
for, while half the Whigs or more are left out.'

1170. Memorandum (1855) by W.E. Gladstone, BL. Add. MSS.44754
1171. J.B. Conacher, op. cit., p. 76
    Gladstone's disapproval of Peel's refusal to endorse a
circular sent by his whip, Sir John Young, to 240 possible
supporters in Parliament at the beginning of the 1847 session -
'It might have been in his power to make some provision for

the holding together and the reconstruction of that great party
which he had reared.... But although that great party was the
work of so many years of his matured life, his thoughts seemed
simply to be "it has fallen; there let it be." A greater idea
still had overshadowed it; the idea of his country now became the
Stewardess of his fame.'

1172. Earl of Malmesbury, Memoirs of an Ex-Minister (2 vols.,
     John Murray, 1884), vol. II, p.54
1173. Robert Blake, The Conservative Party from Peel to
     Thatcher (Fontana,1985)
   Lord Malmesbury to Lord Derby, 15th.December 1856 - 'The
breach which was made in the Conservative body by Peel in 1845-
1846, and which might have been healed to a great degree if
his followers had only given us a fair support or even stood
neutral in the session of 1852-1853, was widened by the formation
of the Coalition Government, on the avowed principle - or no
principle - of discarding all previous party ties.'

1174. Anthony Trollope, Barchester Towers (1857), chap. XXII
   'In politics Mr. Thorne was an unflinching Conservative. He
looked on those 53 Trojans who, so Mr. Dod tells us, censured
Free Trade in November 1852 as the only patriots left among the
public men of England. When that terrible crisis of Free Trade
had arrived, when the repeal of the Corn Laws was carried by
those very men whom Mr. Thorne had hitherto regarded as saviours
of his counctry, he was for a time paralysed.... Now all trust in
human faith must be for ever at an end.'

1175. Lord Stanmore, Sidney Herbert, A Memoir (John Murray,
     2 vols., 1906), vol.II, p. 152
   Sidney Herbert to Gladstone, 13th. April 1857 after
Palmerston's overwhelming victory - 'Furore for Palmerston
lasted far longer in Conservative then in Liberal households.
The regular old-fashioned country gentlemen, who are not
Londoners enough to come within the vortex of the Carlton (CLub)
are Palmerstonians pur et simple, as the only man who can make
peace and ward off deomocracy.... As for ourselves - i.e. Graham,
yourself and me - we are rari nantes, and we are not only broken
up as a party - though I maintain we were not one - but the country
intends us to be broken up and would, I think, resent any attempt
at resuscitation. The fear of the cliques and sections is
universal.'

1176. Philip Magnus, Gladstone (John Murray, 1963), pp. 139-
     140
   Lucy Lyttleton (Gladstone's neice) in her diary, 21st. June
1859) - 'Uncle William has taken office under Lord Palmerston as
Chancellor of the Exchequer, thereby raising an uproar in the
midst of which we are simmering, view* his well-known antipathy
to the Premier. What seems clear is that he considers it right to
swallow personal feelings for the sake of the country.... There
is this question, however - why, if he can swallow Pam, couldn't
he swallow Dizzy, and, in spite of him, go in under Lord Derby? I
don't pretend to be able to answer this.'
* family language meaning 'having regard to.'

1177. John Morley, <u>Life of Gladstone</u>, vol.I, p. 463
     Gladstone at Ormskirk, 1867 - 'Conviction,in spite of early
associations   and   long-cherished   prepossessions   -   strong
conviction and an overpowering sense of the public interests
operating for many, many years before full effect was given to
it, placed me in the ranks of the Liberal party.'

1178. <u>Church Quarterly Review</u>, January 1878
     Gladstone's final verdict on the Peelites - 'Their minds were
eminently just and liberal, but they clung - especially in
foreign politics - to traditions that were outmoded.'

Author Index

The numbers cited are to item numbers, not to pages.

Colvin, H.M., 635
Conacher, J.B., 561, 563, 564,
        1168, 1171
Connell, K.H., 715
Cooper, J.F., 152
Costin, W.C., 178
Creston, D., 377
Croker, J.W., 285, 286
Crook, J.M., 249
Crosby, T.L., 213, 557
Cruttwell, C.R.M., 388
Cunningham, A.B., 247
Curtis, E., 712
Curwen, J.C., 721

Dalling, Lord, 690, 1142
Davies, R., 184, 672
Davies, R.W., 258
Davis, H.W.C., 203, 1144
Dilnot, C., 392
Disraeli, B., 274, 343-349,
        1088, 1143, 1149
Disraeli, R., 273
Dixon, P., 790
Doubleday, T., 191
Dunckley, H., 366
Dudley, Earl of, 287
Dunlop, R., 711

Eastwood, D., 267
Edgcumbe, R., 311
Erickson, A.R.., 565, 568, 571
Esher, Viscount, 913
Evans, E.J., 223, 407
Everitt, G., 625
Eversley, S., 736

Fairlie, S., 55
Feaveryear, A, 424
Feiling, K., 704
Fernandez, T.L., 250
Feutwanger, E.J., 346
Filson, A.W., 181
Finlayson, G.B.A.M., 401, 853
Fisher, D.R., 251, 254, 1016
Fisher, H.A.L., 1162
Fletcher, C.R.L., 599
Flindall, R.P., 182
Foot, M.R.D., 294, 353, 356
Ford, B., 148
Fortescue, J., 387
Francis, G.H., 190
Fraser, W., 839
Froude, J.A., 1107
Fulford, R., 376, 383, 953,
        967, 1009

Garlick, K., 601
Gash, N., 177, 212, 214-
        216, 218, 219, 253,
        260, 364, 365, 400,
        562, 807
George, M.D., 618, 619,
        629
German, B.R., 344
Gladstone, W.E., 294
Glasgow, E., 142
Gordon, A., 570, 572
Gore, J., 283
Gregory, Lady, 296
Gregory, T.E., 421
Greville, C., 187, 297
Guizot, F.P., 192, 929,
        1152
Guyot, R., 429

Halévy, E., 210, 238
        338, 558
Hall, J., 428
Hammond, J.L., 353
Handcock, W.D., 176
Hanham, J.F.C.,171, 179
Hansard, T.C., 323
Hardwick, M., 959
Harris, W., 266, 932
Hart, J.M., 395
Harvey, W., 693
Haworth, J., 657
Hawtrey, R.G., 423
Hayden, M., 718
Hayter, A., 1104
Herries, E., 302
Hibbert, C., 811, 822
Higham, F.M.G., 983
Hill, B.W., 408
Hill, R.L., 399
Hilton, B., 255
Hinde, W., 779, 1000
Hiscock, W.J., 696
Hirst, F.W., 351
Hobhouse, H.,289
Hodder, E., 916
Houseman, J.W., 242
Hoveel, M., 977
Hutchison, S.C., 909
Huelin, G., 797
Huxley, G., 298, 897
Hyde, F.E., 352

Imlah, A.H., 550

Jaggard, E., 264
Jefferey, R.W. 288

Artist Index

The numbers cited are to item numbers, not to pages.

Subject Index

The numbers cited are to item numbers, not to pages.

Albert, Prince, 966, 967, 1007-1010
America, United States of, 934, 986-988, 1022, 1023
Annual Register, 162
Anti-Corn Law League, 1040,1052, 1053, 1098
Ashley, Lord, 943, 980-985

Bank of England, 1018,1019
Beaconsfield, Earl of. See Disraeli, Benjamin
'Bedchamber Incident,' 910-927
Blackwood's Edinburgh Magazine, 163
Bright, John, 656
Brighton, Sussex, 648, 649
Burdett, Sir Francis, 779, 780
Byron, Lord, 691, 692

Canning, George, 329-334, 750, 787-790, 792, 1075-1082
Carlton Club, 651
Chamber Hall, Bury, 632
Chartism, 157, 975-979
Cobbett, William, 161
Cobden, Richard, 969, 970, 998-1002, 1026, 1054-1060,
    1098
Corn Laws, 543-557, 905, 935, 961, 962, 964, 1017,
    1026, 1054-1060, 1098

Daily News, 151, 1061
Disraeli, Benjamin, 960, 1072, 1073, 1143, 1144
Drayton Hall, Drayton Bassett, 633
Drummond, Andrew, 654
Drummond, Edward, 991-997
Dublin, 638, 639,720, 721

Edinburgh Review and Political Journal, 164
Entente Cordiale, 1020, 1021, 1024, 1025

France, 428-430

About the Compiler

LEONARD W. COWIE was senior lecturer in history at both the University of London and the University of Surrey. He has written many books on British history and compiled other bibliographies, including *Edmund Burke, 1729–1797: A Bibliography* (Greenwood, 1994) and *William Wilberforce, 1759–1833: A Bibliography* (Greenwood, 1992).

www.ingramcontent.com/pod-product-compliance
Lightning Source LLC
Chambersburg PA
CBHW060349100426
42812CB00003B/1178